University
of Michigan
Business
School Management Series

INNOVATIVE SOLUTIONS TO THE
PRESSING PROBLEMS OF BUSINESS

The mission of the University of Michigan Business School Management Series is to provide accessible, practical, and cutting-edge solutions to the most critical challenges facing business-people today. The UMBS Management Series provides concepts and tools for people who seek to make a significant difference in their organizations. Drawing on the research and experience of faculty at The University of Michigan Business School, the books are written to stretch thinking while providing practical, focused, and innovative solutions to the pressing problems of business.

Also available in the UMBS series:

Becoming a Better Value Creator, by Anjan V. Thakor

Achieving Success Through Social Capital, by Wayne Baker

Improving Customer Satisfaction, Loyalty, and Profit,
by Michael D. Johnson and Anders Gustafsson

The Compensation Solution, by John E. Tropman

Strategic Interviewing, by Richard Camp, Mary Vielhaber,
and Jack L. Simonetti

Getting Results, by Clinton O. Longenecker and
Jack L. Simonetti

For additional information on any of these titles or future
titles in the series, visit www.umbsbooks.com.

Executive Summary

A variety of trends, including the globalization of business, the increased use of teams, and a change in workforce demographics, have made managing workforce diversity a critical competency for organizations. Developing this competency requires transforming monolithic cultures into multicultural organizations. Many organizations have only recently taken up the challenge; for many others, past efforts have produced disappointing results.

This book presents a model for developing diversity-competent organizations—a model that represents a radical departure from what most organizations have done in the past. The book is a guide to help leaders such as CEOs, members of diversity steering committees, HR professionals, work-group managers, and team leaders to achieve breakthrough results in this difficult and complex area. Numerous examples are presented to illustrate how to apply the ideas contained in the model.

After briefly stating the dimensions of the challenge of diversity (Chapter One), I present the five-part change model along with evidence that the model will *achieve measurable results* in changing the climate for diversity (Chapter Two). The remainder of the book lays out in detail how to implement the five components of the change model. The book will take you through ways to create strong leadership of diversity change efforts (Chapter Three), to leverage research and develop measurement plans (Chapter Four), to create effective ongoing education (Chapter Five), and to align management practices and policies with the goals of multiculturalism (Chapter Six). The book concludes with a discussion of how to follow through to ensure sustainable results (Chapter Seven). Each chapter contains a set of questions designed to provoke thoughtful dialogue and support action planning regarding the ideas presented in that chapter.

Creating the Multicultural Organization

A Strategy for Capturing the Power of Diversity

Taylor Cox Jr.

JOSSEY-BASS
A Wiley Company
San Francisco

Published by Jossey-Bass
A Wiley Imprint
989 Market Street, San Francisco, CA 94103-1741   www.josseybass.com

Jossey-Bass books and products are available through most bookstores. To contact Jossey-Bass directly call our Customer Care Department within the U.S. at (800) 956-7739, outside the U.S. at (317) 572-3986 or fax (317) 572-4002.

Jossey-Bass also publishes its books in a variety of electronic formats. Some content that appears in print may not be available in electronic books.

Library of Congress Cataloging-in-Publication Data

Cox, Taylor.
   Creating the multicultural organization : a strategy for
capturing the power of diversity / Taylor Cox, Jr.
       p. cm.
Includes bibliographical references and index.
   ISBN 0-7879-5584-1 (alk. paper)
1. Diversity in the workplace. I. Title.
   HF5549.5.M5 C688 2001
   658.3′008—dc21

2001000638

Printed in the United States of America
FIRST EDITION
HB Printing   10 9 8 7 6 5 4 3 2

Contents

To my parents: Taylor Cox Sr.,
first mother, Betty Cox,
and second mother, Edith Cox.

Series Foreword

Welcome to the University of Michigan Business School Management Series. The books in this series address the most urgent problems facing business today. The series is part of a larger initiative at the University of Michigan Business School (UMBS) that ties together a range of efforts to create and share knowledge through conferences, survey research, interactive and distance training, print publications, and new media.

It is just this type of broad-based initiative that sparked my love affair with UMBS in 1984. From the day I arrived I was enamored with the quality of the research, the quality of the MBA program, and the quality of the Executive Education Center. Here was a business school committed to new lines of research, new ways of teaching, and the practical application of ideas. It was a place where innovative thinking could result in tangible outcomes.

The UMBS Management Series is one very important outcome, and it has an interesting history. It turns out that every year five thousand participants in our executive program fill out a marketing survey in which they write statements indicating the most important problems they face. One day Lucy Chin, one of our administrators, handed me a document containing all these statements. A content analysis of the data resulted in a list of forty-five pressing problems. The topics ranged from growing a company to managing personal stress. The list covered a wide territory, and I started to see its potential. People in organizations tend to be driven by a very traditional set of problems, but the solutions evolve. I went to my friends at Jossey-Bass to discuss a publishing project. The discussion eventually grew into the University of Michigan Business School Management Series—Innovative Solutions to the Pressing Problems of Business.

The books are independent of each other, but collectively they create a comprehensive set of management tools that cut across all the functional areas of business—from strategy to human resources to finance, accounting, and operations. They draw on the interdisciplinary research of the Michigan faculty. Yet each book is written so a serious manager can read it quickly and act immediately. I think you will find that they are books that will make a significant difference to you and your organization.

Robert E. Quinn, Consulting Editor
M.E. Tracy Distinguished Professor
University of Michigan Business School

Foreword

This book captures the leading-edge theory and practice on how to leverage diversity for the benefit of individuals and the organizations in which they work. Taylor Cox is an unusual combination of scholar and practitioner. He is working on what I consider to be the largest value lever for organizations and for nations today—namely, unleashing all of the human potential that exists in every organization. To do that requires, as a precondition, that individuals find three things in their workplace: that they can say they are treated with dignity and respect, every day; that they are permitted, trained, and encouraged to give their life meaning by making a contribution to the value creation of their organization, every day; and that they are recognized for the contribution they make.

Over the last forty years, in a variety of leadership positions in public and private organizations, this has been my quest. It has been only partly realized, but not for lack of striving. During the past several years, Taylor Cox has been an important partner in this quest, as he has brought his ideas, experience, and energy to Alcoa. Taylor is a demanding partner. Before he agreed to work with us, he spent enough time with our leadership group to be certain that we were serious and that we understood that the achievement of our vision would take time, persistence, and the unflagging support of the leadership. We have made progress, but as Taylor's data demonstrate, we have a long way to go to achieve our vision.

Getting ideas—even great, liberating ideas into practice and ultimately into the genetic code of an organization—is hard, vexing work. Taylor Cox believes, as I do, that the crux of a successful effort can be found in a thoroughgoing systems approach.

Taylor's systems ideas have much in common with the way Alcoa set out in 1987 to become the safest company in the world. Our motivation was to find a way to reach and connect everyone who works for Alcoa with the establishment of a clear, unambiguous, unimpeachable goal: zero safety incidents.

To ensure that our vision was not mistaken for another management scheme to save money, we instructed our financial staff that they were forbidden to calculate the economic value of a safer workplace as we made progress toward our goal. To this day, we have made no such calculation.

We knew that we needed to deal with fundamental elements of human behavior in order to make a real difference, starting with expectations. When we began our effort, we were already the safest company in our industry, by far. In fact we ranked in the top one-third of all U.S. companies in safe performance. But most of our people believed that "accidents happen," that there was an inevitability to being hurt at work, especially in an environment as complex as ours. Liquid metal at 2,000 degrees, huge rolling and cutting machines, and mobile equipment everywhere—these are the everyday conditions in our workplace.

Some of our people believed we couldn't afford to be more safe, so we instituted a policy that we would not spend money on anything else if we had identified projects or repairs that needed to be done to ensure or enhance a safe workplace. By

doing so, we erased the excuse of affordability, directly challenged the so-called "law of diminishing returns," and set a safe
workplace above budget considerations for resource allocation.

Many other actions here contributed to our success: using
universal reporting systems; sharing with our entire workforce
the detailed root-cause analysis of every incident through our
global, real-time information system; using recognition systems;
making benchmarking visits, and so on.

At this writing we have reduced our lost workday incident
rate to the point that, statistically, a person can work for Alcoa
for more than six hundred years without experiencing an injury
that causes absence from work.

Using these ideas, as well as Taylor's model and insights,
will help us accomplish the same kind of world-leading results
in managing diversity. This is a book that is worth your time. I
commend it to you.

April 2001   *Paul H. O'Neill*
                                     U.S. Secretary of the Treasury
                                     Former Chairman, Alcoa Inc.

Preface

I n the early 1980s I began to do research on the effects of diversity of gender, race, age, and other social and cultural differences on human behavior at work. As the work evolved, I came to understand that the implications of workforce diversity were far-reaching and of great importance to the prosperity of organizations, as well as to the pursuit of human happiness. I also came to realize that although the different dimensions of diversity have their own unique qualities and effects, many generic effects and general principles apply to workforce diversity.

In 1993, after ten years of teaching, research, and consulting on the subject, I summarized what I had learned about the dynamics of diversity in the workplace in my first book, *Cultural Diversity in Organizations: Theory, Research & Practice*. The emphasis in that book is on presenting a theory of diversity effects in organizations. Four years later I collaborated with Ruby Beale to write a second book, *Developing Competency to Manage Diversity: Readings, Cases and Activities*. The point of emphasis in that book is to respond to the need for tools to teach about diversity. Although both books include brief attention to the issue of how to change organizations to respond to the challenges of diversity, neither deals with the topic of organizational response in any detail. Moreover, the treatment of organizational change in these books, and in most other books that I have read on the subject, was highly theoretical. Those books laid out in general terms what I *believed* would work to create multicultural organizations, but the ideas were largely untested.

Now, after twenty years of experience with the topic and armed with the measurable results of using my ideas for organization change, I believe the time is right to speak in more detail about how to change organizations to capture the potential power of diversity in work groups. Accordingly, the purpose of this book is to communicate what I have learned from twenty years of working to change companies to welcome and leverage the benefits of diversity. I am moving here from the theory and teaching emphases of the previous books to the *application* of the ideas. Whereas the previous books contain many chapters about the dynamics of diversity effects and one or two chapters about organization change, this book reverses that pattern. It is devoted to helping change leaders understand and use a change process that has been shown to produce positive results.

By *change leaders* I mean people involved in processes to change organizations to become multicultural, that is, to create an environment in which people from all social and cultural backgrounds are respected, where they are able to reach their full potential in organizational contribution and personal goal achievement, and where the power of diversity as an organizational resource is fully captured.

After a brief introductory chapter, this book explains the change model and includes a full chapter on each component of the model. Several features of the book, I believe, make it distinctive. The book

- Offers a systematic, comprehensive model for change
- Provides data on the results of using the model
- Gives detailed examples to illustrate all the main ideas
- Includes discussion of how to involve labor unions
- Includes an integrated case study on managing diversity efforts in one of the world's largest companies (Alcoa Inc.)
- Integrates relevant research via chapter endnotes
- Provides questions in each chapter for discussion and further learning

For me, this book completes a trilogy of contributions about the topic of diversity in organizations: I began with a theory of diversity, then moved to teaching about diversity, and now complete the series by addressing the question, How can we create organizations that are responsive to the challenges of diversity? I do not mean to imply, however, that one must have read the previous two books in order to understand this one. On the contrary, this book is self-contained, incorporating the critical content from the first two books so that readers get the full picture. I sincerely believe that the ideas I share here will help you take a "journey to a different place" on diversity issues.

April 2001   Taylor Cox Jr.
Ann Arbor, Michigan

Creating the
Multicultural
Organization

The Challenge of Managing Diversity

A s we enter the twenty-first century, human capital has taken center stage in the business strategies of enlightened organizations. Attracting, retaining, and effectively using people are increasingly the top priorities of leaders in all kinds of organizations, from high-tech firms to universities, from government agencies to heavy manufacturing firms. In the United States a very tight labor market has intensified the focus on leveraging human capital in recent years. Compounding the challenges posed by more jobs chasing fewer people are additional challenges posed by the increasing diversity of people with the skills to do the work those jobs require.

Consider, for example, the case of gender diversity. In the 1950s three of every four college degrees in the United States went to men; in recent years the majority (around 54 percent) of college graduates have been women. Similarly, in 1971 U.S. women earned fewer than 4 percent of all graduate-level business management degrees; by the early 1990s this figure had multiplied more than sevenfold to around 30 percent. In hot technical fields like engineering, the rates of increase in the participation of women have been even greater.

The shift of worker identity is not limited to gender. Fueled by a variety of factors, including differential birth rates, work groups are increasingly diverse in terms of race and national origin.[1] In addition, more and more organizations are reorganizing work so that it is performed by teams composed of people from different organizational levels and work specializations.

These trends and others, such as increases in the number of working mothers and dual-career couples, make managing diversity a critical competency for today's organizations. Although forward-thinking executives have acknowledged the importance of an effective response to these trends for years, many are finding that the challenges of diversity are not easily met. After more than a decade of work following the clarion calls spawned by the Workforce 2000 report of the Hudson Institute in 1987,[2] many organizations are finding that the goal of creating a multicultural work culture that both welcomes and leverages diversity remains elusive.

This book tells the story of my experience with developing and implementing a process of organizational change for improving the climate for diversity. I do not claim to have all the answers; nor do I claim that the organizations I will discuss as examples have arrived at some final stage of diversity inclusiveness. The work is producing such promising results, however, that it is timely to share what I have learned with others who are embarked on this kind of transformational change.

I am speaking here to those who have responsibility for planning and implementing efforts to manage diversity. Ultimately, this includes all members of an organization, but I especially want to address *recognized leaders* of efforts to manage diversity, from CEOs to members of diversity task forces and steering teams, line managers, and HR professionals. Whatever your level of responsibility, my goal is to help you and your organization meet the challenges of diversity faster and do it more effectively.

Following this introductory chapter, the book is organized as a straightforward presentation of an approach to organizational change. Chapter Two explains the change model and why I believe it has high potential to help organizations. The remaining chapters give details on each aspect of the process, including tips for successful application and warnings of pitfalls to avoid. I conclude with thoughts about the future and words of encouragement for you to join the continuing quest for better knowledge and achievement.

■ Defining Diversity

The term *diversity* has many interpretations. I believe it is neither so broad as to mean *any* difference between people nor so narrow as to be limited to differences of gender and race. Diversity is not another name for affirmative action, nor a name for nontraditional or "minority group" members of organizations, nor a synonym for EEO (equal employment opportunity). Rather, I define diversity as follows:

> Diversity is the variation of social and
> cultural identities among people existing together
> in a defined employment or market setting.

In this definition the phrase *social and cultural identity* refers to the personal affiliations with groups that research has shown to have significant influence on people's major life experiences. These affiliations include gender, race, national origin, religion, age cohort, and work specialization, among others. *Employment and market systems* include churches, schools, factory work teams, industrial customers, end-use consumers, baseball teams, military units, and so on. The geographic scope of the employment-market settings includes local, regional, national, and global settings.

As a characteristic of work groups, diversity creates challenges and opportunities that are not present in homogeneous work groups. By *managing diversity* I mean understanding its effects and implementing behaviors, work practices, and policies that respond to them in an effective way.

■ Problems and Opportunities of Diversity

Although the existence of diversity in the workforce is now widely recognized in organizations throughout the world, it is too often viewed only in terms of legal compliance and human rights protection. In reality the implications of diversity are much more demanding and much more interesting. Increasing diversity presents a double-edged sword; hence the challenge of managing diversity is to create conditions that *minimize* its potential to be a performance barrier while *maximizing* its potential to enhance organizational performance.

Diversity as a Potential Performance Barrier

Theory and research indicate that the presence of diversity in an organization or work group can create obstacles to high performance for several reasons. To begin, diversity can reduce the effectiveness of communication and increase conflict among workers. Compared to more homogeneous work groups, workers in diverse work groups may also experience lower levels of social attraction and display lower levels of commitment to the group. In addition, diversity-related effects such as identity harassment and discrimination behaviors can increase organizations' costs.[3]

As leaders and managers, we may respond to diversity's potential for reducing performance in multiple ways. One is to simply avoid diversity. For example, in his list of eight possible strategies for responding to diversity in organizations, Roosevelt Thomas includes the exclusion of diversity as one option.[4] However, for most organizations, this approach is not only suboptimal—it is not feasible. The reality is that increasing diversity is not a choice but a fact of life. Given this inevitability, one important question becomes, How can organizations increase in cultural diversity without suffering significant adverse effects on performance? Answering this question is one of my goals for this book.

Diversity as Value-Added Activity

The other side of the double-edged sword is that managing diversity well can improve the performance of organizations on a variety of criteria.

First and foremost in the minds of many executives I work with is the criterion of implementing the values of fairness and respect for all people. These values are ubiquitous in formal statements of policy in organizations throughout the world. Too often, however, they are just words on laminated cards that draw snickers from the workforce because they have no real substance. These values will never be anything but meaningless platitudes unless the organization has an effective and ongoing strategy for managing diversity.

Because the achievement of all core values is a key part of the mission of organizations, making fairness and respect for all people a reality is a part of business strategy in its own right, independent of the linkage of these ideals to financial performance. This is an important principle to which I will return at various points in this book.

In addition to fulfilling organizational values, well-managed diversity can add value to an organization by (1) improving problem solving, (2) increasing creativity and innovation, (3) increasing organizational flexibility, (4) improving the quality of personnel through better recruitment and retention, and (5) improving marketing strategies, especially for organizations that sell products or services to end users. If you are involved in organizational change work related to diversity, your work will be greatly helped by an in-depth understanding of these arguments for why diversity is a potential value-added resource. With this in mind, let's explore these connections in more detail.

Problem Solving
First, diversity in work groups can increase revenues through improved problem solving and decision making. Diverse groups have a broader and richer base of experience from which to approach a problem. In addition, diversity enhances critical analysis in decision-making groups. In a series of research studies, Charlene Nemeth found that groups subjected to minority views were better at critically analyzing decision issues and alternatives than those that were not. The presence of minority views improved the quality of the decision-making process, regardless of whether or not the minority view ultimately prevailed. Although Nemeth was studying the effects of minority opinions and not differences of social or cultural group identity per se, the fact that members of minority identity groups often hold different worldviews from majority group members makes this research relevant to diversity in work groups.[5]

The prospective benefits of diversity in problem solving do not necessarily happen by simply mixing people together who are culturally different. Research also suggests that the effect of diversity on the quality of problem solving depends greatly on the extent to which the diversity is proactively managed. In one of the classic studies of this type, Harry Triandis and his colleagues compared the problem-solving scores of homogeneous groups with those of two types of more diverse groups: (1) diverse with training and (2) diverse without training. They found that the diverse groups that were not trained on the existence and implications of their differences actually produced lower problem-solving scores than the homogeneous groups. In contrast, the diverse groups that were trained produced scores that averaged six times higher than those of the homogeneous groups. A similar result was found in some recent research on diversity of ethnicity and national origin.[6] This research suggests that beyond simply diversifying the workforce, organizations need to manage diversity proactively in order to reap its potential benefits for better problem solving.

Creativity and Innovation
Creativity and innovation can enhance virtually all organizational activities. Process improvement, advertising, product design, and quality improvement are examples of organizational activities for which creativity and innovation are especially vital. If there is evidence suggesting that diversity in work teams promotes creativity and innovation, then diversity is a potential resource to improve these important organizational activities. I will cite a few examples of such evidence.

In her 1983 book *The Change Masters* (Simon & Schuster), Rosabeth Moss Kanter notes that high levels of innovation occur in companies that

- Have done a better job of eradicating racism, sexism, and classism

- Tend to have workforces that are more diverse with respect to race and gender
- Are more deliberate than less innovative companies in taking steps to create heterogeneous work teams

In a similar vein, research on educational institutions in the late 1970s shows that the most innovative schools are also the most tolerant of diversity.[7] My own research comparing ethnically diverse teams to all-Anglo teams doing a marketing task shows that the diverse teams outperformed the homogeneous ones by about 10 percent.[8]

Organizational Flexibility

The existence of diversity and the adaptations organizations make to accommodate it should lead to greater flexibility. One way that diversity can make organizations more flexible is through changes in the patterns of employees' cognitive structures, that is, their typical ways of organizing and responding to information. For example, there is some evidence that women tend to have more tolerance for ambiguity than men—a quality that has been linked to both higher levels of cognitive complexity and the ability to perform ambiguous tasks.[9] Similarly, studies on bilingual and monolingual cultural groups in various nations have shown that bilingual individuals tend to have higher levels of cognitive flexibility and of divergent thinking than monolinguals. Because diversifying the workforce increases the presence of people who speak two or more languages, it indirectly increases flexibility of thought.[10]

The responses an organization makes to diversity can also lead to greater flexibility as a kind of by-product. For example, broadening policies and reducing standardization tend to make the organization more fluid and adaptable. This increased fluidity should allow the organization to respond to environmental changes faster and at lower cost. Although this line of reasoning is somewhat speculative and not based on research, the logic seems compelling.

Human Talent
Given today's increasingly diverse labor market, organizations that are best at attracting, retaining, and using the skills of diverse workers will enjoy a competitive advantage. To illustrate this point, consider the analogy of making a fruit salad for some very important guests. Assume that you are selecting fifty pieces of fruit from five categories: apples, oranges, pears, strawberries, and peaches. In each category there is a full range of quality to select from but a limited number of pieces available. You naturally want the finest pieces so that the salad will be superb. If you select only one type of fruit—let's say apples—the range of quality will be 1–50. As the available amount of fruit is limited, some of the fruit will be of mediocre quality. However, if you select only the ten best pieces of fruit from each of the five categories, the salad will be much better.

Labor markets operate similarly, particularly when the rate of unemployment is low. Organizations that are effective at attracting, retaining, and using people from only one or two social-cultural groups will be at a disadvantage compared to those that are equally effective with people from a variety of backgrounds. This is a quality issue because the capabilities of employed people are a major raw material in all organizations. When the average quality of this crucial input falls, we can expect one of two consequences: (1) either we work harder to get the same outputs as competitors who have a higher average quality of inputs or (2) we accept lower levels of outputs. This is exactly what is happening today, but these effects are often masked by the complexity of factors that affect the ultimate performance indicators of organizations.

Marketing Strategy

An important consequence of the rising globalization of business is that consumer markets, like the workplace, are becoming increasingly diverse. An automobile manufacturer in Japan cannot afford to ignore the fact that nearly half of all new-car buyers in the United States are women, regardless of the gender composition of car buyers in Japan. Likewise, no reasonable person in the consumer goods industry can afford to ignore the fact that roughly a quarter of the world's population is Chinese or that immigration to the United States from mostly Asian and Latin American countries is occurring at the rate of more than one million people per year. In the United States, Asians, blacks, and Hispanics now collectively represent nearly $500 billion annually in consumer spending. Because research on consumer behavior has consistently shown that sociocultural identities affect buying behavior, marketing success will depend, to some degree, on the ability of companies to understand and respond effectively to the cultural nuances of the diverse marketplace.[11]

A well-used, diverse workforce can facilitate selling goods and services in the increasingly diverse marketplace in several ways. First, there is a public relations value in being identified as an organization that manages diversity well. Second, marketing efforts may gain from the insights of employees from various cultural backgrounds who can assist organizations in understanding cultural effects on buying decisions and in mapping strategies to respond to them. Third, broadly representative employees can help create strategies to enhance customer relations when working with people from a diversity of cultural backgrounds.

This brief review of some of the pertinent research makes the point that managing diversity well can lead to better results on a variety of performance dimensions. Achieving these results, however, requires that organizations manage the complex challenges of diversity far more effectively than most firms have been able to. Why past efforts have often fallen short is the subject of the next section.

■ Why Past Efforts Have Failed

Although recognition of the potential problems and benefits of diversity has increased in recent years, many organizations have been disappointed with the results they have achieved in their efforts to meet the diversity challenge. A case in point is Alcoa Inc. When I was asked in December of 1996 to begin working with Alcoa's corporate diversity committee, the message to me went something like this:

> We have been working on improving our company to include and utilize the full skills of people who are different from our traditional workforce for many years, but despite what seems to us like a lot of effort, we still have a workforce that is dominated by white, U.S.-born men, and our progress in moving people of other backgrounds into top positions in the company has been very slow. In addition, we continue to get feedback from the workforce, including some of our highest-ranking women and nonwhite men, that the company is not very hospitable to people who come from different social and cultural backgrounds than our traditional workforce. What are we doing wrong? How can we move this to another level of accomplishment?

Does this sound familiar to you? If it does, I am not surprised because my contacts with hundreds of managers from dozens of companies in recent years tell me that Alcoa is far from alone in its frustration about less-than-hoped-for results on diversity goals.

I have learned that there are three main reasons why many past efforts have been disappointing: (1) misdiagnosis of the problem, (2) wrong solution (that is, failure to use a systemic approach), and (3) failure to understand the shape of the learning curve for leveraging diversity work.

The lessons I have learned about achieving breakthrough results in managing diversity will be presented in the upcoming chapters. To set the stage for those discussions, let's briefly examine these three sources of past failures.

Misdiagnosis of the Problem

The root cause of many failures to manage and leverage diversity is a misdiagnosis of the problem. The problem posed by diversity is not simply that there are not enough people of certain social-cultural identity groups in the organization. Nor is it primarily one of making insensitive people more aware that identity matters, although this is certainly a part of what needs to happen. Bigoted and insensitive people do exist, and they are a significant barrier to the presence of diversity and to realization of its benefits, but this is a very superficial diagnosis of the problem. The more significant problem is that *most employers have an organizational culture that is somewhere between toxic and deadly when it comes to handling diversity.* The result is that the presence of real diversity is unsustainable as a characteristic of the organization.

Let me say more about what I mean by *real* diversity. Research has shown that differences of social-cultural identity such as gender, national origin, race, and work specialization represent real differences in *culture.* These group identities should therefore be regarded as micro-culture groups.[12] Organizations, however, tend to hire people who are perceived as fitting the existing culture of their firm. Moreover, because many organizations deal with cultural differences by exerting strong pressure on new employees to assimilate to existing organizational norms (acculturation by assimilation), real differences tend to diminish over time.[13] Due to the pressure to conform, members who have high cultural distance from prevailing norms of the work culture tend to either leave the organization or modify their thinking—

and their behavior—to achieve acceptance. The result is that apparent differences of cultural groups, such as an increasing presence of women, may represent only small differences in worldviews.

The presence of a diversity-toxic culture is the ultimate cause of the failure of organizations to successfully embrace diversity in its members. Once you identify the problem in this way, you are more likely to avoid the other two main reasons for past failures to manage and leverage diversity.

Wrong Approach

The second major reason for past failure to manage diversity effectively is the selection of the wrong approach to meeting the challenge of diversity. This mistake follows directly from the failure to accurately diagnose the problem. In the typical case, the problem diagnosis is limited to "insufficient diversity," and the solution consequently focuses on changing inputs to the system. This involves such actions as creating multifunctional and cross-level work teams, placing foreign nationals on the board and in key developmental assignments in the host country, and recruiting more women and racial-minority men. There is no question that this change in the composition of human inputs is an important step toward changing the culture, especially if the changes include positions of high decision-making authority. However, this is only one element of the system. Systems theory tells us that the elements of a system are highly interdependent so that change in one element requires adjustments in all the others if the system is to function effectively (and, I would add, if the new elements are to survive and prosper).[14] Unfortunately, the approach of new inputs has usually not been accompanied by corresponding changes in the other elements of the system. The result is a predictable suboptimization or even outright failure of the change effort.

Here is a simple example to illustrate what I mean. Recruiting is an element of the organizational system that has received great emphasis in past efforts to manage diversity. A typical scenario in the United States is that the organization makes an effort to hire more racial minorities and women for management and professional jobs. However, as the hiring criteria remain otherwise unchanged, the organization continues to hire and promote people who have a low tolerance for working with women and racial-minority men. The result is that the cultural minority hires encounter unnecessary barriers to contribution that at best are overcome with extra effort and at worst lead to turnover or subpar job performance. Extend this logic to other system elements, such as employee development, performance appraisal, compensation, mentoring, and so on, and you can begin to see the startling implications.

What organizations need, therefore, is an approach to change that aggressively pursues the deliberate and knowledgeable alignment of all other elements in the system with the changes in human inputs. This concept of *systems alignment* will be illustrated throughout the book and is especially prominent in Chapter Six.

Misunderstanding of the Learning Curve

The third major reason for past failures is misunderstanding the shape of the learning curve for leveraging diversity. Here I use the term *learning curve* in a broad sense to capture the development of the organization and its members toward competence to welcome and use diversity as a resource. Leaders often act as though the learning curve is steep, with the achievement of a high level of competence occurring after only a few months or a year of concerted effort. On the contrary, I have found that the learning curve on diversity work is much flatter, requiring years of conscientious effort to achieve a high level of proficiency. For example, at the time of this writing, my work with Alcoa is entering its fifth year, and yet there is general agreement that many areas of the company are still in the early stages of the curve.

When leaders make the mistake of acting as though a flat learning curve is steep, their behavior becomes dysfunctional. They become impatient about seeing results, tend to shift their focus to other things, and prematurely withdraw attention to the process being used to create change. All of these responses are deadly to the prospect of creating real, sustainable change.

This point highlights once again how important it is to diagnose the problem accurately. Misdiagnosis leads to the wrong approach for action and the wrong timetable for seeing results. In addition, I challenge you to be sincere about what you are doing when you tackle the challenges of diversity. Leaders often say they understand that creating a welcoming climate for diversity is a culture change and requires years of intense effort, but their actions contradict their words. For instance, if after just one year of work, progress on diversity is no longer a topic of significant discussion when business plans are reviewed, this sends the wrong message about priorities and suggests a naïve notion of what it takes to institutionalize diversity competency.

Of course, meeting the challenges of diversity involves more than correctly diagnosing the problem and having the will and determination for long-term commitment to the effort. Those who lead this change work must know how to go about the process of changing the organizational culture. The next chapter presents a model to meet this need that is already producing measurable results.

CHAPTER SUMMARY

Even though theory and research suggest that diversity can be a resource to enhance organizational performance, there is a crucial distinction between merely having diversity in the workforce and developing the organizational capacity to leverage diversity as a resource. The challenge of diversity is not simply to have it but to create conditions in which its potential to be a performance barrier is minimized and its potential to enhance performance is maximized.

The challenge can be simply stated, but sustaining an effective response is complex and difficult. Past efforts have often fallen short for three main reasons: (1) failure to recognize that the central problem is the presence of a diversity-toxic organizational culture, (2) a consequent failure to take a systems approach to meeting the challenge of diversity, and (3) the mistake of thinking that the learning curve is steep rather than flat. Avoiding these shortcomings and achieving better results is a formidable task. Nevertheless the stakes are high, especially in countries like the United States that feature high levels of cultural diversity, a democratic political tradition, and legal and value systems that place great emphasis on fairness, respect, and equal opportunity. How organizations can effectively meet the challenges of diversity is the subject of the remainder of the book.

Questions for Further Learning and Development

1. What is wrong with this statement: "I have a diversity person for you to consider for your general manager job"?
2. Can the term *diversity* be defined too broadly? Why or why not?
3. Which of the arguments presented in the chapter on why managing diversity is a high priority for organizations apply to your organization? Which is the single most compelling argument?
4. If you have been involved in managing diversity efforts in the past, have the results met your expectations? If not, do any of the three most frequent reasons for failure cited in the chapter apply?
5. What steps can you take, alone or with the support of others, to reduce or prevent the three most frequent causes of failure cited in the chapter from blocking your efforts to manage diversity effectively?

A Strategy for Meeting the Challenge

magine that you have just been appointed to serve on a diversity steering committee for your company and that your group is charged with creating an approach to managing diversity for your organization. The results of your work will be presented for approval to the CEO of your company or, if you work for a mid-size or large company, the CEO and his or her direct reports. This is the first meeting of the group, and you are all staring at a blank piece of easel paper wondering where to begin.

What the group needs is a comprehensive conceptual model that identifies the main activities needing attention and shows how the activities relate to one another. Such a model provides a basic planning and control tool and brings coherence to what otherwise would likely be fragmented efforts. If you are working in a large organization, you want the model to be sufficiently detailed to give direction yet maintain enough flexibility to be customized for differences in local operations.

In this chapter I present an overview of a model for organizational change that I believe meets the needs of your steering committee. It responds to the need for a systems approach to managing diversity, as described in Chapter One. Here I introduce the elements of the model, present background on its development, and give information about the results that I have achieved in applying it in organizations.

■ A Model for Cultural Change

Figure 2.1 depicts a model for organizational change as a response to the challenge of diversity. In this section I briefly define the components of the model; subsequent chapters address each in depth.

An effective organizational change effort should include all of the elements depicted in this diagram. As the flow of the arrows suggests, the change effort cycles through all of the elements and is continually assessed and refined over time in a process of continuous loop learning.

Leadership

In the context of organizational change, leadership is behavior that establishes a direction or goal for change (a vision), provides a sense of urgency and importance for the vision, facilitates the motivation of others, and cultivates necessary conditions for achievement of the vision. Leadership is the most essential element for change; without it, nothing happens.

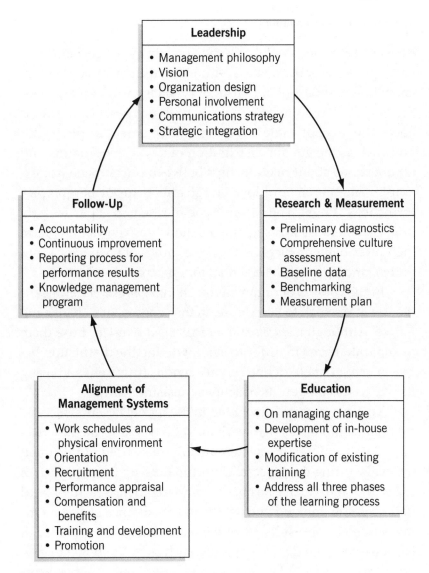

Figure 2.1. **Change Model for Work on Diversity**

Research and Measurement

Research is the purposeful collection of data by which we can answer questions about some environmental element or phenomenon. In the context of organizational change work on diversity, the questions tend to be primarily of two types: (1) questions about the level of some environmental element or phenomenon such as the gender distribution of a work population and (2) questions about relationships between phenomena (for example, whether an employee's age affects his or her job performance ratings). The second type of research is particularly important because investigating relationships allows us to make high-probability predictions about the causes of phenomena, and understanding causes is essential for effective intervention.

In the context of organization change, *measurement* means the use of research to keep score on the progress of a change initiative. Although *research* and *measurement* overlap, I use them as separate terms in order to acknowledge the distinction between using data to define action agendas (research) and using data to assess the results of actions (measurement).

This component is included in the model because successful organizational change work must be well informed by relevant data, with results systematically measured at pertinent intervals during the process. Unfortunately, up to now much of the work on diversity has been hampered by a dearth of hard data to guide thinking and action and an absence of systematic measurement of results. Where measurement has occurred, it has too often been done myopically, such as by limiting it to government-requested EEO numbers. Chapter Four suggests ways to overcome these shortcomings.

All organizations, regardless of size or type, need to include both research and measurement as necessary elements of their change processes. Of course, the types of research and measurement must be customized to fit the setting. For example, an important measurement for consumer products companies is market share in niche markets that are defined in terms of identity groups like "women" or "Asians" or by geography such as "the China market." But this type of measure would not be appropriate in developing a diversity change effort for a state government or in a copper company. Likewise, employee survey research on diversity-related behaviors such as racial stereotyping can be useful in diagnosing the organizational climate for diversity in the United States, but in Mexico you might research stereotyping on the basis of region of origin rather than race.

Education

When is the last time you saw a major change introduced in your organization without an intensive effort to help people learn new information and skills? If you can think of one, chances are the initiative was not successful. Education is a central feature of any change effort. I use the term *education* in preference to *training* to signify my conviction that learning must be approached through a variety of methods. For example, I find that many organizations drastically underuse personal coaching as a means of educating people about diversity.

Although there has been a great deal of activity in the area of diversity training, early returns on its effectiveness are not encouraging.[1] In Chapter Five I share what I have learned about how to do diversity education more effectively.

Alignment of Management Systems

I use the term *management systems* broadly to include any organizational policy, practice, rule, or procedure. This covers the major HR activities like recruitment, promotion, and development, as well as other conditions such as work schedules or the design of the physical work environment. All these systems must be aligned with the goal of leveraging diversity.

The fulfillment of this component in the change model requires a fairly deep understanding of diversity and its effects. To illustrate this point, consider the following incident, which took place in a recent leader training session of a Fortune 100 company.

A group of about thirty-five high-potential managers were gathered for a two-week leadership development experience that included a half-day session on leading change related to diversity. One of the attendees asked the company's executive vice president of human resources, "Have you seen people either promoted or specifically held back from promotion in our company based on an assessment of their competence for dealing with diversity?" The vice president responded that he had not seen either. The implication of the question, and rightly so, was that if diversity competency was to be a high priority in the company, it should be a criterion in the promotion decision process. The fact that this had not occurred indicates that this organization, like most others, had not yet fully integrated diversity into its management systems.

Interestingly, I find that many organizations recognize the need for experience and depth of expertise and thus seek outside help for diversity training while eschewing help with work on aligning systems. One reason for this is failure to recognize that organizations are social systems and thus require the alignment of all key elements. When this part of the change process gets short shrift or is omitted altogether, the result is that the overall goals of the diversity effort are not realized.

Follow-Up

This component involves implementing action, establishing accountability for results, and capturing and recycling the learning so that the action steps become more and more precise. This component overlaps with all the others but is linked especially to the research and measurement component.

■ Origins of the Model

The model I have described is essentially a process of transformational change applied to the challenge of managing cultural diversity in organizations. The ideas on which it is based are taken primarily from previous work on transformational change, open systems theory, and revolutions in science.

From work on transformational change, I have drawn on ideas about how transformational leadership differs from transactional leadership.[2] One of the most important differences is that the latter puts emphasis on overseeing and coordinating tasks within an existing vision and philosophy, whereas the former involves guiding the organization to a new vision. Also, transactional leaders preside over incremental change, whereas transformational leaders usher in revolutionary change.

Open systems theory helps us understand how the components of organizations are interdependent—hence the need for a comprehensive approach to change and for careful attention to the alignment of policies and practices with the goal of the change effort. The fact that the model has five components and includes the idea of continuous-loop learning (signified by the arrows in Figure 2.1) may be traced to systems theory concepts.[3]

From work on revolutions in science comes the assumption that preparing organizations to have and leverage diversity requires fundamental change in the ways of thinking and acting that define the organization's culture. Especially important here is Thomas Kuhn's book, *The Structure of Scientific Revolutions*, which highlights the need for fundamental shifts of thinking about assumptions and relationships. Two examples of how Kuhn's work applies to the change model are (1) the idea that diversity has the potential to add value and not just to disrupt performance and (2) the centrality of education as a vehicle to bring about paradigm shifts. As Kuhn writes: "At times of revolution . . . the scientist's perception of his environment must be re-educated in some familiar situations, he must learn to see a new Gestalt."[4]

Starting from these basic ideas on how change occurs, I have refined the model with learning from other early writers on the topic of diversity in organizations[5] and from my work with companies such as Exxon, Ford Motor Company, Eli Lilly, and Phelps Dodge. The experience of using the model's ideas in these companies produced important refinements in the content of the model, as well as some indications of its usefulness for changing organizations. But by far the best test of the model to date comes from work begun in 1996 with Alcoa. The next section presents some early results from this experience.

The Alcoa Experience

Breakthrough achievements start with good ideas, but ultimately it is the testing of ideas with measurable results that establishes their value. Throughout this book, I discuss my experience with Alcoa to illustrate using the change process just presented to meet the challenge of managing diversity. I want to emphasize that this is very much a work in progress, and I am not holding Alcoa up as an established benchmark of world-class achievement on diversity. What makes this example useful is that Alcoa has clearly taken a "journey to a different place" on diversity issues in the last few years as a result of using the ideas from the model for change. As indicated by data I will present shortly, early results from those parts of the organization that started work with the model in early 1997 are very encouraging. These results were achieved by a sustained effort of leadership, measurement, education, alignment of policies, and follow-up by many dedicated people. In many ways it is their story that is being told by the Alco case example in the book.

Alcoa is the world's largest producer of aluminum, serving a global marketplace in industries such as packaging, automotive, aerospace, and construction. The company is organized into dozens of autonomous business units with more than two hundred operating locations and well over one hundred thousand employees in nearly thirty countries. The nature of the business with employees and customers around the world is one factor making an effective approach to managing diversity essential to the success of the company's business strategy.

In late 1996, then-CEO Paul O'Neill commissioned a corporate steering committee to research and develop an approach to the diversity challenge that would produce breakthrough results for the company. Working with input from the heads of all Alcoa business units and resource units, the committee recommended adopting the change process that I had developed. This recommendation was approved by the corporate executive council; as a result the model outlined in Figure 2.1 was sent out as a template for worldwide use under the sponsorship of CEO Paul O'Neill and President Alain Belda.

Under the leadership of senior executives George Bergeron, Mike Coleman, John Pisse, Al Renken, and Joe Haniford, two core businesses of Alcoa—the rigid packaging division (RPD) and primary metals (PM)—pursued the first field tests of the process. These business units were selected in part because they were thought to be among the most difficult in which to produce real change (a belief that was later borne out by baseline climate assessment data). Prospects for positive change were also dampened by a poor work relationship between leaders of the main labor unions and the leaders of management. We thought that if some progress could be made in this part of the company, it would bode well for successful application of the process in other business units.

In early 1997 I led a team of consultants to visit two locations of the RPD and PM business units and completed a miniassessment of the current work culture. We relied heavily on employee feedback to assess aspects of the culture relevant to diversity. Following this diagnostic work, the management teams in the two locations, working with leaders of the local

Steel Workers of America organizations, developed and implemented an action plan that applied ideas from the change process to address the gaps of culture found in the baseline assessment. I met monthly with the leadership groups of both organizations to help them craft the plans and discuss progress on implementation. The plans featured multiple steps for each of the five change model components.

After roughly eighteen months of implementation work, we completed a follow-up assessment to determine the extent to which feedback from the workforce on the quality of the climate for diversity in the organization had changed. Tables 2.1 and 2.2 present some examples of the data from this change measurement work.

Overall, in location 1, forty-three of forty-four measurements improved between the baseline and the 1999 update. The average improvement was around 8 percentage points and, as you can see from the Table 2.1 data, many measures showed a dramatic improvement. In location 2, of twenty-six measurements used in both 1997 and 1999, twenty-three improved, with an average improvement of 12 percentage points.

These data tell a story of remarkable progress in units that many insiders said would be the hardest to change. Along with the progress represented in the tables, these organizations have also made significant progress in increasing the representation of women and racial minority men in the workforce, including increases in management jobs, and they have dramatically improved the quality of the union-management relationship.

In addition to the data from these two organizations, I got interesting results from another analysis using data from thirty-seven of Alcoa's manufacturing locations. In this analysis I computed correlations (a test of degrees of association among variables) between measures of the climate for diversity and measures of the productivity and work quality of the plants. A positive correlation suggests that organizations with a more

Table 2.1. Data on Results of Climate Change at Alcoa Location 1

Measure	% Favorable Response[1]		
	Baseline (1997) %	Update (1999) %	% Change
Mistakes are tolerated as vehicles to learn and support risk taking.	38	52	+37
I have the same opportunities here as others of my ability, experience, and education.	49	64	+31
Communications are good here between management and hourly workers.	28	42	+50
I would recommend this company for employment to a good friend.	45	64	+42
There is tension here between men and women.*	65	75	+15
Communications are good here between whites and racial minorities.	69	82	+19
Employees feel free to express differences that may be due to different cultural backgrounds.	54	65	+20
My supervisor is sensitive to my personal and family situation.	62	76	+22
There is frequent stereotyping of people based on their work area.*	45	62	+38
There is frequent stereotyping here of people in the lower job grades.*[2]	46	60	+30

[1]A favorable response is agreeing with a positive statement or disagreeing with a negative statement. Negatively worded items are noted by an asterisk. No opinion responses are excluded.

[2]Stereotyping was defined as assuming a person has limited abilities or negative traits based on one's membership in a *specified* culture group.

Table 2.2. Data on Results of Climate Change at Alcoa Location 2

Measure	% Favorable Response[1]		
	Baseline (1997) %	Update (1999) %	% Change
Mistakes are tolerated as vehicles to learn and support risk taking.	47	51	+9
I have the same opportunities here as others of my ability, experience, and education.	39	53	+36
Communications are good here between management and hourly workers.	32	40	+25
I would recommend this company for employment to a good friend.	37	57	+54
There is tension here between men and women.*	50	65	+30
Communications are good here between whites and racial minorities.	54	78	+44
There is frequent stereotyping of people based on their work area.*	28	52	+86
There is frequent stereotyping here of people in the lower job grades.*	37	58	+57

[1]A favorable response is agreeing with a positive statement or disagreeing with a negative statement. Negatively worded items are noted by an asterisk. No opinion responses are excluded.

[2]Some items from location 1 are not repeated here because they were not used in the location 2 baseline measurement.

positive culture for diversity also achieved better performance on these key manufacturing metrics. The results of this analysis are shown in Table 2.3.

The data in Table 2.3 indicate that the relationships between measures of diversity climate on three dimensions of diversity are positively associated with measures of workforce productivity and quality. I am especially encouraged by the fact that, despite the small sample size, three of the six correlations in Table 2.3 are statistically significant.

Table 2.3. Correlations on the Relationship Between the Diversity Climate and Key Measures of Plant Performance

Diversity Climate Measure[1]	Work Performance Measure	
	Productivity	Work Quality[2]
Gender Index	.25	.57*
Race Index	.16	.57*
Work Function Index*	.41*	.16

*Diversity dimension = differences of department

**Correlation is statistically significant

[1]Indices are based on averaging the percent favorable response on survey questions that measure three dimensions of diversity climate: (1) amount of stereotyping behavior, (2) amount of intergroup conflict related to culture-group differences, and (3) quality of communications between people of different groups.

[2]Due to missing data for one or more measures, the effective sample size for the productivity analysis is 25 and for the work quality analysis is 15.

Because I have seen measurable change occur using the ideas for managing diversity presented here, I am encouraged to share with you what I have learned in hopes that it will be helpful to others who are facing similar challenges. At this point you may be wondering whether ideas found to be effective in a large multinational company are applicable to a firm that differs from Alcoa in size, scope, type of products and services, or other factors. Ultimately, you will be the judge, but my experience tells me that the basic process given here will work for any organization. Of course you will need to customize the process to fit your circumstances. In this regard keep in mind that the two manufacturing organizations where we piloted our work in Alcoa are only about 2,500 people each in size. Most of what they achieved was accomplished without any extensive support from the corporate office. Indeed, we were well on our way to implementing the change model in this business unit before the formal roll-out of the model to the rest of Alcoa occurred in January of 1998.

Make no mistake, achieving results like those shown in the three tables is hard work, and the job is never done. The leaders of the two units of Alcoa featured in the table would be the first to tell you that they neither consider themselves to have all the answers nor feel that they have "arrived" at the goal of multiculturalism. Nevertheless, they are proud to have accomplished something that is rare in the annals of diversity work: measured movement of a culture to a significantly higher level toward an established vision. Inspired by these results, their work continues with the highest expectations of further progress.

CHAPTER SUMMARY

Managing and leveraging diversity requires a process of deep organizational change. The model presented in this book draws on work from social science, the natural sciences, and organization science to create a change process for transforming organizations to a new level of achievement of diversity goals. The process recognizes that real change in this area will require a systemic approach toward an ultimate goal of institutionalizing a new culture—one that welcomes diversity and allows all members to use their skills and abilities to achieve their full potential in pursuit of business and personal goals. Data from my experience with applying the change model in one of the world's largest companies show significant progress in changing the culture to a different place on diversity issues. I hope I have whetted your appetite to hear more. The next five chapters discuss in detail how to use the model, with the specific action steps that led to these impressive results.

Questions for Further Learning and Development

1. How does the process model described in the chapter compare to what has occurred in your organization up to the present time?
2. Using the model as a guide, what are your organization's greatest strengths and most glaring weaknesses?
3. Take a minute to review the data presented in Table 2.3 and answer these questions: (1) What are the limitations of this kind of research? (2) What kind of research could be done in your organization for a useful study of the connection between the organizational climate for diversity and organizational performance measures?

Leadership

The First Requirement
of Change

When I started working on a diversity change effort with Exxon Research and Engineering Company, I met early on with the company president, Terry Koontz. In that meeting he told me four things that still stand out to me as one of the best expressions of strong leadership that I have encountered.

First, he shared his *vision* for the work. He summarized his vision by saying that his goal was to significantly improve the company's ability to hire, retain, and use people from all social and cultural backgrounds and to improve the performance of the organization by tapping the full potential of the entire workforce.

Second, he indicated that he was *personally committed* to doing what was necessary to increase the company's capacity to manage diversity. The required changes in behavior, he asserted, would start with him.

Third, he explained in detail how the management of diversity was *strategically integrated* with the existing objectives of the business. In this regard, he stated that managing diversity would be one of the top three business objectives for the company and noted the linkage between achieving excellence in managing diversity and achieving a world-class quality of work. He further explained that managing diversity was "the people side of quality." This meant that diversity would not be treated as an "add-on" to the portfolio of things that were already being done in the area of managing people. Rather, it was to become an umbrella under which everything the company did with regard to managing people would occur.

Finally, he communicated his decision that there would be changes in the *organization structure* in order to support the high intensity of effort that would be needed to successfully launch the change effort. Specifically, his head of HR, Tom White, would be spending no less than 50 percent of his time as coordinator of the diversity work for the foreseeable future. Further, a steering committee composed of some of the most respected people in the company was being formed to create a detailed diversity plan.

This one meeting touched on four of the six elements of leadership excellence in managing diversity that are addressed in the change model shown in Figure 2.1, namely, (1) creating a vision, (2) being personally involved (to demonstrate required new behaviors), (3) establishing the right organization design, and (4) integrating diversity work with the company's business strategy. Unfortunately, this example of the beginnings of effective leadership is countered by numerous examples of inept leadership behavior that has plagued organizational efforts to improve the management of diversity.

In this chapter, I first address the question, Who are the leaders of change efforts when it comes to work on diversity? Then I expand on the four elements of leadership that were emphasized in my meeting with Terry and discuss some of the lessons learned about effective leadership from my work with him and many others engaged in this kind of effort. Although the two other elements of leadership mentioned in the model—creating a management philosophy and a communication strategy—are also important, I focus here on the four specified elements in order to keep the chapter to a reasonable length and because these latter two elements overlap to some degree with the other four.

■ Who Are the Leaders?

Before talking about the required behaviors and responsibilities of leaders, it may be useful to address the question of who the leaders are in work on diversity. In many respects the answer is, *anyone who has influence with other people.* However, for the most part, my focus in this chapter is on people in one of the following categories:

- CEOs
- Heads of units of organizations (divisions, business units, departments)
- Diversity officers and coordinators at any organization level
- Members of diversity steering committees, councils, and task forces
- HR staff members with assignments on diversity
- Heads of labor unions (national, regional, local)

I want to elaborate on three things about this list: (1) leadership starts at the top, (2) it takes many leaders to make the change effort work, and (3) leadership cannot be delegated.

Leadership Starts at the Top

To be fully effective, leadership on diversity *must* start at the top. In this regard the importance of strong leadership by pioneering CEOs like John Houghton at Corning, Robert McAlister at

U.S. West, Jim Preston at Avon, David Kearns (and later Paul Alair) at Xerox, and, more recently, Ernest Drew at Hoechst Celanese is now legendary. These companies have established themselves as leaders on diversity work in no small measure due to the strength of leadership at the top over a period of many years—leadership that has been passed on in the succession planning process to ensure continuity of attention.

To further illustrate the importance of leadership commitment at the top, let me give you two personal examples from companies I have worked with. One is a mid-sized insurance company, where we started work in the mid-1990s by completing comprehensive assessments of the work culture in five of the firm's business units. I met with the company president and received his personal assurance of commitment to follow up on the data with action steps and frequent communication to the employees on progress. However, before we had completed the initial data collection phase of the work, this man resigned from the company, reportedly over a dispute with the heads of a new parent company. We ended up presenting our results to the new president. According to insiders, this person did little or nothing to implement our recommendations or take other action steps to respond to the data. As a result, seven years after starting the process, this organization remains stagnant in terms of achieving diversity excellence.

My second example comes from work with a mid-sized research and engineering company. A change of presidents after I began working there in 1989 produced a noticeable slow-down in progress toward the goals that were laid out for diversity excellence. Although several members of the leadership team below the CEO level, including the head of the HR function and several engineering managers, continued to work on the diversity change effort, the effort lost momentum that was never recovered. The fact that this very promising change effort, using the same model that was presented in Chapter Two, achieved only minor results, was, in my view, largely attributable to the loss of strong CEO leadership that occurred after only one or two years of work.

To guard against this kind of derailment of the change process, it is essential for CEOs to place a high priority on commitment to excellence in managing diversity in the succession planning process for their own job and those of other key leaders of the organization.

It Takes Many Leaders

Having made the critical point about the value of strong leadership at the top, let me quickly add that commitment at that level is a necessary but not sufficient condition for effective leadership on managing diversity. Success requires many leaders. In Alcoa, for example, the remarkable progress that has been made in several of the company's core businesses is the result of tireless efforts by leaders at various levels of the management chain, as well as officers of the major labor union and various members of change teams devoted to managing diversity. For example, in 1999 executive vice president George Bergeron included an assessment of progress on the diversity goals of the company as part of the incentive compensation formula for all managers reporting to him. Partly as a result of this action, the business units under his authority were all active in working the change model and achieved remarkable progress in the first year of work. In another business unit, a diversity steering committee composed of mostly line managers from various regions of the firm led the organization through the first steps of culture assessment and into action planning, including leadership education for six of their largest operating locations.

Perhaps my favorite example of the point that "it takes many leaders" is the experience of working with leaders of the local 304 of the Steel Workers of America in Knoxville, Tennessee.

When I first met with these union leaders and presented the idea of working together with management on a change effort on diversity, they came close to walking out on me. The local president was unambiguously, and very vocally, opposed to taking even the first step in the process (collecting employee data). However, through many weeks of talking and looking at preliminary data from the workers of the organization—data telling us that diversity issues existed in the plant—we arrived at a partnership in which these union officers have been highly supportive of the process and instrumental in our success (see data from location 1 in Table 2.1).

This example makes the point that leadership is a cooperative effort. The message for you is to be a coalition builder. When you can identify a network of middle managers, key individual contributors (for example, engineers, software designers, librarians, faculty members, and so on, depending on the nature of your business), and, where appropriate, leaders of the hourly workforce who are prepared to show leadership on managing diversity, your chances for success will be greatly increased.

Leadership Cannot Be Delegated

Although my list of categories of leaders for work on diversity includes diversity officers and members of the HR staff, I include them with an important caveat, namely that responsibility for making change happen cannot be delegated to persons in these roles. *Extensive experience tells me that unless it is clear that the CEO of your organization and heads of your main operating units have primary responsibility for breakthrough progress on diversity, your change effort is doomed to failure.* Diversity officers and HR staff have a crucial role to play as facilitators of change, but they cannot be held responsible for making it happen.

Here are some signals that will tell you where your organization is on this point. First, check the composition of your diversity steering groups or task forces. They should not have more than one or two representatives from the HR function. Second, the chair of your main planning group should not be an HR person or a diversity officer. This is especially applicable in organizations where the HR function is not a full strategy partner at the top or where the head HR person does not report directly to the CEO. Third, if you are using consulting help, the lead consultant for the work on diversity should have access to, and be in contact with, key operational leaders in your organization. If this person is limited to talking through the HR organization or diversity officer, then you haven't established the right concept of leadership.

Let me elaborate on this third point to give you a better feel for the general principle of nondelegation of responsibility for change. In the mid-1990s a large multinational company in the automotive industry initiated a change effort on diversity. I was asked to work with a high-level steering group, which included a virtual "who's who" of recognized leaders in the business. Although I met these people and worked with them during the monthly meetings, outside the meetings my contact was expected to be confined to people in the HR function. When I began to express resistance to what I perceived to be too much control by the HR staff, the consulting relationship was discontinued. Coincidentally, I was recently discussing the progress of this company toward changing the culture with a number of employees who are evening students in my MBA class at the University of Michigan. According to them, the company's progress, despite a high activity level, has been incremental and not revolutionary.

In contrast to this scenario, during my work at Alcoa I have been in contact with a wide range of high-level line leaders, including presidents of business units and CEO Alain Belda. My first involvement as a consultant in Alcoa was facilitated by an HR person but actually established with Al Renken, then general manager of two of their largest plants. This difference in point of contact for me as the lead consultant goes hand in hand with Alcoa's other efforts to place responsibility for change squarely and unambiguously in the hands of operations heads and not with the corporate office or staff groups. I am convinced that this difference in philosophy of leadership is a major reason Alcoa is showing measurable progress on change, whereas a number of other companies, after the same length of time, are not.

■ Defining a Vision for Change

Dwight Eisenhower is reported to have said, "Leadership is the ability to decide what is to be done and then get others to want to do it."[1] The ability to decide what is to be done is one way of expressing the leadership requirement of *vision*—a picture of what needs to be accomplished—along with some general guidelines about how to go about it.

Visions for managing diversity should tell us some characteristics of an organization that welcomes and leverages diversity. To test yourself on this, complete the following sentence: "If we are successful in creating a multicultural organization that truly values diversity, our company will _____."

This exercise forces you to be specific about what success looks like. For example, one answer I often give is that a multicultural organization is one in which people of all cultural backgrounds can contribute and achieve to their full potential in pursuit of organizational and personal goals. Such an organization will

- Include a mix of people of various cultural and social backgrounds at all organization levels
- Use pluralism and not assimilation in acculturating new members

- Include people of all cultural and social backgrounds in informal networks and mentoring
- Eliminate bias (for example, prejudice, stereotyping, and ethnocentrism) based on identities such as gender, national origin, race, and other social-cultural factors
- Minimize intergroup conflict among people based on differences of identity

Each of these carries with it implications for action. For example, consider the call for *pluralistic acculturation*. Imagine that your organization is growing, in part, by acquiring other companies and that these companies' cultures are distinctly different from your firm's culture. When the assimilation mode of acculturation is used, integration teams focus almost exclusively on bringing the acquired firm up to speed on the key strategies and operating methods of the acquiring firm. For example, in the case of recent acquisitions of Kawneer company and Alumax by Alcoa, this included extending to these firms a knowledge of specific Alcoa expectations and processes for financial reporting, safety, and production systems. There is general agreement that much of this knowledge transfer has improved the ability of the acquired companies to compete in their respective businesses. There is less agreement, however, on the extent to which Alcoa has been consistently open to the possibility of learning from the acquired firms.

A two-way approach to knowledge transfer is one of the hallmarks of pluralism. Under pluralism, integration teams spend time understanding the culture and operating methods of *both* organizations and thinking carefully and thoroughly about such questions as (1) Where does the entering organization need to conform to existing norms of the acquiring firm and where can it be left free to create its own norms? and (2) What can the acquiring firm learn from the acquired firm about practice improvement in various areas?

Being specific about vision provides a sense of direction for the people you are trying to lead. It also frames, at least in a general way, what has to be measured to determine whether or not the change effort is working. For example, in the vision of multiculturalism that I provided earlier, one thing to be measured would be the level of access and the quality of mentoring received by people of different social and cultural backgrounds.

As the quotation from Eisenhower implies, effective leaders don't just create visions by dictation, that is, by saying, "Here is what we're going to do." Instead, they have a strong sense of where the enterprise needs to go and some sense of how to get there, but they recognize that they won't get there unless they can light a fire under the people with whom they have influence to embrace this vision for change. What is needed, therefore, is an ability to create a *shared* vision for diversity. Based on my experiences with leaders at Alcoa and elsewhere, I have found the following to be very helpful in getting others to share your vision:

- Demonstrate some personal passion for the needed change.
- Provide a compelling case for why it is the right vision.
- Communicate profusely.

■ Setting a Personal Example of New Behaviors

In verses 4 and 5 of the seventh chapter of the Bible's book of Matthew we find the following admonition:

> Why do you behold the splinter that is in your brother's eye, but not consider the log that is in your own, or how will you say to your brother, let me pull out the splinter from your eye, and yet a log remains in your own eye? You hypocrite, first cast out the log from your own eye and then you will see clearly to cast out the splinter from your brother's eye. [modified King James version]

This classic advice fits squarely among the most important elements of effective leadership for managing diversity change work. Nothing kills the ability to lead faster than hypocritical behaviors. If the change effort is to succeed, the norms of behavior in the organization must change, and leaders must be the first to demonstrate this shift of behavior.

Because it is important for leaders to model the new behaviors, it is necessary to identify behaviors that distinguish diversity competence from incompetence. Some of the ways in which leaders must illustrate diversity-competent behaviors are obvious. For example, no one would take seriously a diversity change process led by someone who is prone to sexual harassment behaviors. However, lots of much more subtle behaviors need to be looked at as well. For example, consider the following case, which is based on feedback from employees of an organization where my colleagues and I recently completed a diversity climate assessment. As part of their managing diversity effort, the organization decided to conduct training on workplace harassment with an emphasis on sexual harassment. The organization is about 85 percent male, and there were indications that the environment was especially difficult for women. The local operations head or the head of HR was kicking off each of the training sessions. At the first session, which was attended by the person reporting the incident to us, the operations manager opened the meeting by thanking the people for attending and then reportedly said, "I'm sorry you have to be here today and sit through all of this." The employee relating the story, who happened to be a woman, stated that she and others immediately tuned out, and the potential value of the session was lost before it started.

Here is another example. The CEO of a large company is speaking more and more often on the subject of diversity, emphasizing value to the business, and urging the managers of the firm to give it their attention. The messages are on target, but some people have noticed and commented on the fact that when he talks about what managers have to do, he always refers to "he" and never "she." Many leaders are unaware that they are inadvertently communicating that it is business as usual regarding diversity, even when discussing the topic directly.

A third example comes from a comment made by a member of the board of directors of a multinational company. This woman is reported to have asked a member of the company during an informal conversation, "How could a Brazilian be appointed to the job of president of the company?" The not-so-subtle implication, of course, was that this U.S. company should not be run at the top by foreigners.

These and countless other anecdotes illustrate that many leaders have a long way to go to set the right example for managing diversity culture change. Toward this end, let me leave you with three additional ideas. First, if your organization is using formal job performance appraisals and if valuing diversity is included as a rated behavior, this is a good place to start in cataloging diversity-competent behaviors for use by leaders. If your organization does not have a "valuing diversity" or similar performance factor, consider adding one.

A second suggestion is to take advantage of available diversity-competency assessment tools. Several such tools are available, including my "diversity competency profile instrument," which identifies twenty-five specific diversity-supportive or antidiversity behaviors.

Finally, Table 3.1 lists additional examples of behaviors that demonstrate leading by example and showing a personal commitment to the change process. This list is a sample of behaviors I have observed while working with dozens of managers at various levels in my recent work with Alcoa.

The examples in Table 3.1 illustrate positive leadership behaviors that set a good example for others in the organization and send a message that the work on diversity is indeed a high

Table 3.1. Examples of Strong Leadership Behaviors

1. A general manager personally conducts feedback meetings to present the results of an assessment of the organization's climate for diversity.

2. A high-level manager who has been assigned to serve on a business-unit diversity steering committee is scheduled to attend the first meeting of this group. The committee has invited a senior outside consultant to attend this meeting and help them kick off their work. After the meeting is scheduled, this manager is asked by his supervisor (the head of the operation) to attend another meeting out of town on the same day. The manager insists that he cannot attend the meeting with his supervisor because he must attend the diversity steering group meeting. The operations GM accepts this and excuses him from attending the out-of-town meeting.

3. While attending a training session for leaders of diversity change work, the president of the business unit notices that some of his direct reports who are attending the meeting are not focused on the business at hand (they are whispering to one another about a business problem unrelated to diversity). During a break, the president calls these people aside and gives them a firm reminder of the importance of refocusing their attention on learning about diversity.

4. The top management team at a manufacturing plant commits to kick off and close *every* session of diversity awareness training. This requires three people to share responsibility for a total of one hundred training sessions conducted over a ten-month period, including sessions occurring during the midnight shift.

5. The vice president of human resources of a business unit personally designs and delivers a series of short seminars teaching principles about managing diversity, based on the book written by the lead consultant for their change process. His plan is to provide ongoing education by teaching a different portion of the book at each of their leadership meetings over an extended period of time.

6. The president of the local Steel Workers Union works with the general manager of a manufacturing operation to create a video to express their joint commitment to the change process for creating a positive diversity climate.

7. The CEO of the company agrees to be interviewed by a middle manager to discuss his views on people issues, including diversity. The interview is videotaped and distributed to all business units for use in introductory education.

priority. Although I have seen many such examples, I have also witnessed many examples of poor leadership. You can start a list of ineffective leadership on diversity by simply reversing the items in the table. To illustrate, consider item 2 of Table 3.1. Many times I have seen managers renege on their commitment to attend a meeting dealing with the work on diversity in order to accommodate a demand for that time period that arose *after* the diversity meeting was planned. The message, which is not lost on the people who are influenced by such a manager, is that the work on diversity has relatively low priority. Incidentally, notice that item 2 in Table 3.1 actually exemplifies strong leadership behavior for both the manager and his or her supervisor because the operations head could have insisted that his direct report drop plans to be at the diversity steering committee meeting to attend the other one. The fact that he didn't is a very significant aspect of this example.

A second illustration concerns item 3 in Table 3.1. Although I observed the positive leadership noted in the table first hand, I have also been involved in many training sessions on diversity at which high-level managers or union leaders not only failed to keep others focused on the training but allowed themselves to be interrupted during the session to attend to other business. In some cases this has been extreme. For example, one union president who committed to attend a two-day training class actually participated in only about half of the training time. In another case, an HR staff member was charged with learning some training content so that it could be taken back to others in her organization. She left a planned five-day train-the-trainer session on the third day.

If you have been involved in organization change work, you have no doubt observed the great truth in the adage that, to be effective, leaders must "walk their talk." Too often leaders fail to do this, but when they do, their actions indeed speak louder than their words. Demonstrating commitment to change by personal action sends a strong message. But either doing the wrong things or simply doing nothing also sends a message. It behooves us to ask ourselves whether we are consistent in the messages our own behavior sends with regard to diversity.

■ Defining a Structure to Plan and Coordinate Change

In addition to creating a shared vision and demonstrating their personal commitment, leaders of the change effort must create an organizational structure to shepherd the change process. I will discuss the most widely used structure first and then address alternatives to this industry norm. The best approach for you will depend on a variety of factors, including your organization's size, industry, and culture.

Larger organizations have typically organized for change work on diversity by appointing a full-time corporate officer for diversity. In most cases, the people in these high-visibility jobs have a small support staff of two or three people. These officers are often supported by coordinators for diversity in various operating units of the firm. Examples of organizations that have used this model include General Electric, Shell Oil, and Motorola. In all of these companies the diversity officers report directly to the CEO of the company. I believe this reporting structure is far superior to those in which the highest-ranking person with specialized responsibility for diversity work reports to someone other than the CEO or COO of the organization.

Another staple of organizational structure for diversity work in large companies is the appointment of a corporate-level steering committee. This group, which typically serves for the first eighteen to twenty-four months of the change effort, is charged with creating a strategy and tools for managing diversity and with serving as expert resources to facilitate the implementation of the strategy in the field units of the firm. For example, when the work on managing diversity as a culture change process started at Ford Motor Company in 1993, an executive diversity council was appointed that included many of the most powerful people in the company: Bill Ford (now chairman of Ford), Ed Hagenlocker (then head of North American Operations), and executive vice president of human resources, Pete Pestillo, among others. Other organizations have chosen to staff their enterprise-level steering groups with people at slightly lower levels of the management chain. For example, when Shell Oil started its change effort on diversity in 1995, the company commissioned a group of middle-level managers to work as a task force. I worked with this group on forming a diversity strategy, which they presented to CEO Phil Carol and his direct reports. The principle to take away from these examples is that the enterprise-level steering teams should be staffed with people who are highly regarded and have some significant decision-making authority in the organization.

Local diversity task forces or advisory groups often support the enterprise or corporate-level steering groups. For example, in the RPD of Alcoa, the Warrick Plant of twenty-five hundred people has a diversity advisory committee. This is a group of about eight people appointed by the operations manager, together with the local union heads. Both salaried and hourly people serve on the committee, which meets at least monthly to evaluate results on completed action steps and discuss ideas for further advancing the change process on diversity in the plant. Periodically, the committee meets with the operations head and his or her direct reports to maintain communications and present recommendations for next steps. The group is also used to keep the line-management leaders informed about developing issues related to diversity. Among other benefits, this additional source of information can be helpful in identifying and diffusing workers' concerns and conflicts *before* they become discrimination lawsuits.

In my view, neither designated full-time diversity staffers nor enterprise-level steering groups should be permanent in a company. They should be used to facilitate the launching of change initiatives, which normally takes two to three years. If the work is done with appropriate focus and priority, this will be long enough to complete the launch of the work and mainstream the functions of planning, coordination, control, and communication. By *mainstream* I mean that these functions are performed within the normal job duties of other employees rather than within a specialized "diversity" function or task group.

One caveat to this advice is that the plug might be pulled too soon on the diversity officer position. My recommendation to eliminate the role after two to three years is based on an assumption of an intensive effort toward change. If you eliminate specialized diversity staffing in your organization before some level of institutionalization of the action steps has occurred, lasting changes are unlikely to materialize. For example, in a multinational pharmaceutical company where I did some work in the mid-1990s, the role of corporate diversity officer was eliminated after less than two years of work. In her place an enterprise-level steering group was established, but the velocity of the work was never the same after this change of structure; to date the company has not achieved the goals of the change effort.

In contrast to full-time diversity personnel and steering committees, it is wise to maintain some kind of diversity advisory group as a standing committee. When these groups work effectively and are taken seriously by the senior leadership, their value-to-cost ratios can remain high as a long-term staffing mechanism for diversity work.

Criteria for Diversity Teams

Regardless of the size or type of your organization, you will want to include some type of diversity planning committee in your leadership team for diversity work. These teams have various names such as diversity steering committee, diversity action team (also known as DATs), and diversity council. For the enterprise-level version of these teams, the group is normally charged with creating a diversity business plan or strategy, serving as a resource to units within the firm, and monitoring the progress of change. I am often asked for suggestions on the composition of these teams. The following criteria should be considered:

- Highly respected and knowledgeable
- Personal interest in the work and a desire to serve
- Knowledge about diversity or a high motivation to learn about it
- Willingness and ability to invest a significant amount of time in the work
- Diversity of members on gender and other dimensions of difference that are salient in your workforce

Definitely avoid the following in forming diversity planning teams:

- Making it too big (more than ten people is too many)
- Homogeneity of membership on diversity dimensions that are most visible in your organization
- Exclusion of majority group members (for example, at Exxon Research and Engineering, the inclusion of white male engineers was a must)
- Over-representation of HR people (no more than two)
- Assignment of people with no credibility on the subject of diversity

The last of these items warrants elaboration. You want to be sure that the people in designated leadership positions on diversity have a good reputation for working with people who are different. A way to accomplish this is to take an informal poll of a *diverse* group of people who have worked with potential appointees. In one organization where I worked, a supervisor who had been reprimanded for borderline harassment behaviors was placed on a diversity committee. For many people this had the effect of undermining the perceived seriousness of purpose of the effort.

Alternative Structures

Thus far, I have described a proven method for large firms to organize resources to move forward a change agenda for managing diversity. However, I do not mean to imply that there is one best way to organize. For example, if your firm employs fewer than two or three thousand people, you probably do not need a full-time person to coordinate the launch of the change effort. Indeed, even some large companies have launched a corporatewide change process for diversity without the benefit of specialized diversity staff. One such company is Alcoa, where the effort has thus far been overseen by the existing management structure in the various business units, in addition to a network of diversity steering committees and task forces. This approach has the advantage of facilitating the mainstreaming of work on diversity and making it clear that ultimate accountability rests with the company's operating leadership. But there are also drawbacks. Most notably, the pace of change is often slowed when no one has full-time accountability for diversity efforts. A second problem is difficulty with transferring knowledge about what is learned about managing diversity from one part of the organization to another.

Another alternative structure is illustrated by the organization of the Exxon Research and Engineering Company, a firm of about twenty-five hundred employees. In that case the top HR person in the company was expected to spend at least half his time on the diversity effort. He was assisted by a corporate steering group of about ten people and by various percentages of time from his own staff. For example, two of his direct reports were assigned to work with external consultants to design and deliver diversity awareness training.

Regardless of what structure is used, it is important that the top leaders in your organization take responsibility for creating staffing at an appropriate level of time commitment to ensure that the change effort is adequately resourced. In my experience, this often does not occur and is a major cause of failure. If, for example, your company elects not to have designated diversity staff, it is imperative that the people who are assigned to do the work to launch the change effort (such as diversity planning team members) are freed up from certain other responsibilities so that they can devote significant blocks of time (a minimum of 15 to 20 percent of their workload) to launching the diversity change effort. You want to avoid the all-too-common mistake of simply adding responsibility for launching a change effort on diversity to the list of duties of HR staff members and line supervisors who are already overworked due to the fallout from downsizing.

■ Achieving Strategic Integration

One of the most serious sources of failure or suboptimal results for diversity change work is the failure to successfully integrate the work on diversity with the strategy of the firm. Here is a short quiz to help you determine whether this is a problem in your company:

Can leaders in the organization explain specifically why success at managing diversity will help with the accomplishment of the firm's main business objectives?
Is it widely understood that the time horizon for high-priority work on diversity is longer than one or two years?

Can leaders explain in clear terms how managing diversity fits
with other key initiatives of the people strategy of the firm?
Are there mechanisms for communication and shared learning
among people and groups working on various aspects of
the strategy for managing people?
Is the strategy for managing people well integrated with the
other components of the overall organization strategy?

If you answered no to any of the questions, then you have
work to do on strategic integration. Some help on how to do this
integration is given in the following sections.

Diversity and the Organization's Mission

The first type of strategy integration that must occur is that of
diversity strategy with the overall mission of the organization.
For example, in universities this means explaining why having
students and faculty of different genders, national origins, reli-
gions, races, and so on has the potential to improve the quality
of teaching and research. For a hospital it means specifying why
having medical professionals of different identity groups can improve the quality of health care delivery.

For profit-making companies, the task also involves clari-
fying the impact of managing diversity on profitability (general
ideas about the content of the linkage between performance and
the management of diversity were given in Chapter Two). The
challenge for leaders is to clearly communicate the details of
how the potential performance benefits of diversity specifically
apply to your organization. Unfortunately, too many leaders do not
do their homework and therefore cannot provide more than a
superficial explanation of the link between managing diversity
and the overall goals of the enterprise.

Once they are comfortable with the content, leaders must also
take the initiative to actually deliver the message. This must be
done often and with conviction.

Time Horizon

One of the important implications of this discussion of strategic integration is that establishing goals and action steps for managing diversity is a part of *strategic* planning. It should therefore involve a long-term time horizon for development and implementation of the levers of change. Once again, I find that although many leaders give lip service to the idea of a long-term effort, actions suggest that a flurry of activity for twelve to eighteen months is sufficient. To dispel this notion, one requirement of leadership is to communicate the expectation, both by words and actions, that the journey to multiculturalism is a long one.

For large organizations, I recommend that leaders think and plan in terms of two- to three-year cycles. The first cycle should take you through the launch of the change effort. The second cycle should fully establish diversity as part of the ongoing work of the organization, which I like to refer to as the institutionalizing of diversity competency. If all goes well, an organization can aspire to achieving genuine benchmark status by the end of the third cycle. The notion of two- to three-year cycles is also suggested because it coincides with the defined timeline for long-term planning in many organizations. Also, the idea of taking six to nine years to achieve benchmark status is consistent with the seven- to ten-year timeframe that is often discussed as the required timeline for changing the culture of an organization.

For smaller firms, the timeline I've just discussed may be abbreviated somewhat because small size facilitates a faster pace for both the planning and the implementation of an organization change agenda. Even here, however, the proper time horizon for the work must be specified in terms of years and not months, and there must be a commitment to ongoing attention.

People Strategy as Business Strategy

Another aspect of strategic integration is the placement of the strategy for managing people within the strategic framework for bottom-line business results. This means making clear the priorities for managing people that are required in order to make the other aspects of the business strategy such as financial, marketing, and technological plans achievable. For example, at the time I was working with Eli Lilly in the mid-1990s, the company had defined its business strategy in terms of three main areas: critical capabilities, global presence, and targeted disease control. The "critical capabilities" item in turn had six components, among which was to establish "preeminent organizational effectiveness." This item covered the need to establish and maintain a world-class organization of people with the skills and competencies that would make the other elements of the strategy possible. Similarly, Alcoa has defined five key business processes: financial, environment, health and safety, manufacturing processes, and customers and people. Once the place of strategies for managing people in the overall business strategy is well established, the stage is set for inclusion of the work on managing diversity.

Managing Diversity as People Strategy

The fourth requirement for strategic integration is to ensure that the work on managing diversity becomes an integral part of the overall strategy for managing people in the organization. The most straightforward way to achieve this is to specify managing diversity as a formal component of the people strategy. To illustrate, recall that establishing preeminent organizational effectiveness was a component of one of the three main elements in the Lilly business strategy for 1995. Their diversity change process was developed as part of the planning work for achieving preeminent organization effectiveness. One way that managing diversity helps the company achieve preeminent organization effectiveness is by increasing its chances of being able to successfully recruit and retain the best people in the world.

Although managing diversity was primarily developed as part of the organizational effectiveness component of strategy, it was linked secondarily to the strategic aims of global presence and targeted disease control. For example, by learning about diversity and using the insights of a diverse workforce, the company is better able to develop and market medications for use with a diverse consumer base. This view is supported by emerging research showing that cultural background factors like ethnicity can affect such things as how patients react to medications.[2]

At Alcoa, leveraging diversity is one of four specific goals within the business process for managing people. Specifying the linkages among strategic components in the manner illustrated by these two examples creates a strategic architecture that helps employees, stockholders, and others to readily understand how the work on diversity fits into the big picture of the mission and strategic thrust of the organization.

Once a strategic architecture is formed, much of the actual work to integrate the diversity change process with other elements of people strategy will be done by the HR function. The work involves taking a look at what else is going on in the organization regarding the management of people and making sure that the planning and action steps for managing diversity are interwoven with those needed for these other "people" goals. In most organizations it is not difficult to identify the other elements of people strategy that need to be considered. To illustrate, when I was working on culture change with Phelps Dodge in 1995 and 1996, the company was doing a lot of work on implementing teams and also was beginning to work aggressively on strengthening its capability for employee development. The diversity work fit naturally and tightly with these other goals, but it took a concerted effort to make sure that the integration actually occurred.

To give an example in production settings: training on teamwork often emphasizes problem-solving techniques, interpersonal communications, and concepts of synergy and work-group interdependence. What is often missing is explicit attention to team members' differences and their potential impact on the functioning of the team.

Here is another illustration of effective people strategy integration. At about the time Alcoa was developing its diversity change process, the company was also working on revising its processes for recruiting new college hires and experienced hires for management and professional jobs. Recognizing the importance of integrating this work with the work on managing diversity, HR manager Harold Shields and others worked hard to ensure that criteria related to diversity were heavily represented in the revised criteria for hiring. One specific is that diversity of the student body and attention to diversity in the educational program were made one of six or seven criteria that were used to formally rate colleges and universities to create a short list of preferred schools for on-campus recruiting. This example brings to mind the final element of strategic integration: mechanisms for communication and coordination.

Mechanisms for Communication and Coordination

In the example just given in which the recruiting plan and the plan to manage diversity were integrated, the integration was greatly facilitated by the fact that Harold Shields served on both the corporate diversity steering team and the task force working on the recruiting plan. This approach of "overlapping membership" is one of the most effective mechanisms for ensuring that the people working on various aspects of the people strategy are talking to each other on a regular basis.

Another step that Alcoa took to cement the cross-communication among different people initiatives was to have several different task forces working on various elements of people strategy report their work to the corporate diversity steering committee. As mentioned earlier, this was a high-level group that included three business unit presidents, the executive vice president of HR, and the second-highest-ranking person in the finance organization, among others. Because the same people were overseeing the work of all the task forces, they could provide a critical integrating function for the work on people strategy in the organization.

In small organizations, integration is easier. For example, in my work with the Warrick and Tennessee Plants of the Rigid Packaging Division of Alcoa, the lead team, composed of the operations general manager and his or her direct reports, serves as the people strategy team for the organization. Integration is assured because one group works directly on all phases of the people strategy, including diversity. As explained previously, an advisory group of people at lower levels researches ideas and provides recommendations for action to the lead team. Organizations that have appointed a diversity officer should assign the tasks of communicating and coordinating the diversity work with other aspects of the people strategy to that role.

Regardless of how it is done, it is the responsibility of senior leadership to see that this type of integration happens. Failure to do so will result in misalignment within the people strategy and also lost efficiency. As a simple example of misalignment, consider the combination of recruiting plans and diversity plans. You could easily end up with a list of universities for college recruiting that produces a very homogeneous pool of candidates, which would make the effort to increase diversity in management and professional jobs more difficult. Efficiency can be lost because of missed opportunities to leverage activity undertaken to support achievement of one "people" goal to help other goals.

For example, as we do our diversity climate assessments we routinely include questions on other goals so that the results of this activity have multiple uses. In contrast to this practice, I often find cases where organizations are using two or three different surveys from different consultants in the same timeframe, with no communication between them. Leaders have a responsibility to ensure that this kind of inefficiency is minimized.

When the task of strategic integration is done well, employees are not prone to view the work on diversity as the new "flavor of the month" and approach it with the kind of half-hearted effort that accompanies the thought that *this too shall pass*. Although these linkages may seem obvious to some people in your organization, they will not be to most employees, and thus it is necessary to make them explicit and to maintain constant communication about them. It may also be necessary to adjust them as the other elements of the business plan change over time.

CHAPTER SUMMARY

Strong leadership is the single most essential component of the change process for managing diversity. In this chapter I have identified leaders and offered a philosophy of leadership in which leadership starts at the top, effective change requires many leaders, and leadership cannot be delegated. Four aspects of leadership were discussed in detail: creating a vision, demonstrating personal involvement, creating an organizational structure, and achieving strategic integration. Attention to the suggestions discussed here for the fulfillment of these four elements of leadership will go a long way toward making your effort to manage diversity successful.

Questions for Further Learning and Development

1. Keeping in mind the insights from this chapter, evaluate the extent to which the CEO of your organization is demonstrating strong leadership on managing diversity.

2. If the leadership at the top is not strong, what are the causes? What can you do, perhaps with the support of others, to strengthen the leadership of your CEO and other top leaders?

3. How have you organized for managing diversity in your organization, or how do you plan to do so? What assignments of authority and responsibility have occurred or should be undertaken? If work is already under way, is the structure effective? If not, what is missing?

4. Where is your organization on strategic integration according to the quiz in the section entitled, "Achieving Strategic Integration"? (Note: deduct 20 percent from 100 for each no answer). If your score is lower than 100 percent, what can be done to improve it?

5. What can you do to strengthen your own leadership of the effort to create the multicultural organization?

Leverage Research, Develop Measurement Plans

One of the key principles of the approach to change advocated in this book is that change must be *data driven*. As this admittedly overused phrase has many different meanings, I will be clear about its use in this context. To that end, in this chapter I will discuss ideas for the following uses of data in the change process for diversity competence: (1) how to use data to build a commitment to change, (2) how to use data to enhance diversity education, (3) how to diagnose the climate for diversity, (4) how to measure progress, and (5) caveats for using research to drive change.

■ Using Data to Build Commitment

Any type of change encounters resistance—some types more than others. My experience with change to create a welcoming environment for diversity suggests that there is more than the usual amount of resistance and that resistance is especially likely to come from majority culture group members. One reason for this accelerated resistance is fear among majority group members that change will produce a zero-sum game in which others gain and they lose. For example, in many U.S. companies, the EEO aspect of diversity work is interpreted by some people as employment gains for women and racial-minority men at the expense of the traditional power group, white men. In mergers and acquisitions, attention to diversity is sometimes viewed as taking control away from the more dominant partner in the merger in order to enfranchise members of the smaller partner. In organizations with labor unions, diversity work is sometimes viewed by managers as tilting the balance of power in favor of the unions—and so on.

This form of resistance is at least partly due to a misunderstanding of what the diversity work is all about. One way to overcome this type of resistance is through education and communication designed to show that when implemented insightfully, developing competence for diversity has long-term benefits for everyone. Resistance also occurs when people do not see the need for intervention around diversity issues. Many people in organizations simply don't see that there is a problem to be solved or an opportunity to be realized when it comes to workforce diversity. This is where the use of research can create a breakthrough. The sections to follow present three examples of this use of data: (1) developing the business case, (2) getting executives focused on the need for change, and (3) promoting a shared leadership with labor unions.

Developing the Business Case

My first example comes from work with Shell Oil. In 1995, Shell created a task force to develop an approach to diversity that would take the company to a higher level of achievement. This small group of people met frequently in the "war room," where they assembled an impressive array of resource materials and laid out their ideas on newsprint taped to the walls. One of the first and highest-priority tasks was to build a "business case" showing why investment in a change effort related to diversity was closely linked to the company's financial success. They first developed their conceptual logic: diversity competence was critical for effective teamwork, would increase the quality of human inputs to the firm, and so on. Then, working closely with me as a consultant, they put together internal and external data in support of these arguments. Finally, they created their intervention strategy. When their report was presented to the executive council of the company, the team was able to win support for virtually all of their recommendations. The well-articulated business base, using hard data, was an important part of their success.

Although this example involves a large, privately owned company, the development of a business case, using the approach just discussed with relevant data for the particular organization, can work equally well for any type of organization. To illustrate, consider a small law firm. A part of the conceptual framework for the business case might be that the demographic profile of potential clients is changing to include more people who were born in Mexico or the Far East. The data would document the magnitude of the change in the ethnic profile among potential clients and the relevance of these shifts for the firm's business. This might include demonstrating the market potential of these non-traditional customer groups and presenting evidence that certain aspects of providing high-quality legal services are likely to be different to fit this change in clientele. The intervention strategy might include hiring lawyers and staff of Latino and Asian descent, holding language classes, and conducting cultural awareness education. The specifics are different than they were at Shell, but the process is the same.

Getting Executives Focused on the Need for Change

Development of a business case for diversity is only one form of using data to increase commitment to the change effort. To illustrate with a different example, I will draw on the work at Alcoa. Nearly everyone who was present agrees that a watershed event in terms of leader commitment was the meeting of business unit presidents and resource unit heads in the fall of 1997. At this meeting data were presented on the climate for diversity, based on surveys and interviews at four or five locations of the company. Quotations taken from interviews with employees of all job grades were written on easel paper and displayed around the walls. The leaders then "walked the wall" and read the messages, many of which testified to behavior and conditions that grossly undermined the company's core values and policies. The impact of this simple experience with internal data on the subject was phenomenal. This meeting was clearly a galvanizing event for building support of the change effort at Alcoa.

Using Data to Promote Shared Leadership with Unions

Another example of using data to build commitment, also taken from experiences at Alcoa, involves union leadership. One of the themes of this book is that where unions exist, participation by union leaders in the change work on diversity can make an enormous difference in the success of the work. When we started working in one business unit of Alcoa, the sentiments of the local union leadership ran from neutral to strongly antagonistic. As noted earlier in Chapter Three, in my first meeting with him, the president of the local union was strongly resistant to the managing diversity effort. However, through a series of subsequent meetings at which data collected from this work location were presented, support from the union gradually increased. Clearly, the presentation of these data alone did not produce the improvement in the working relationship that has taken place there, but it was a major factor.

A breakthrough event in this case occurred when the union president asked to see the results of the recently completed diversity climate assessment for the hourly workforce only. He questioned the extent to which the data, shown earlier on the total workforce, applied to hourly workers. His suspicion was that if there were any diversity-related issues to be addressed at the plant, they were among the salaried workforce or in transactions between the hourly workers and their supervisors. What the data clearly showed, however, was that most of the diversity-related issues applied equally to salaried and hourly members of the organization. My colleagues and I produced the necessary "hourly only" report and presented the results to the top leadership of the union. Subsequently, we presented these same data to a meeting of all the department stewards of the union. This use of research data helped the president and other union leaders make the decision to give strong support to the intervention efforts to improve the climate for diversity in the plant. At this writing, they are continuing to follow through on this commitment.

Even if your organization does not have a union, you may encounter resistance from members of the workforce in lower-level jobs who simply see this work as the responsibility of management and not the total organization. Using data to show that the issues to be addressed involve behavior by members at all levels can be an effective way to remove some of this resistance.

■ Using Data to Enhance Education

A second way of using research data to promote organizational change related to diversity is to include it in education efforts. This takes various forms. One way is to use feedback from employees about specific issues of the diversity climate to create case scenarios for analysis in training courses on diversity. Doing so has several advantages. First, it responds to a widespread request among people working on diversity education to bring the learning down to the level of behavioral change. The use of cases allows learners to apply what they are hearing to solve a problem. Second, it provides scenarios that are guaranteed to be relevant to the group being trained and thus avoids the often-encountered learning obstacle of "that doesn't happen here." Still another benefit is that you are likely to save training design costs because the material is available from another step of the change process that you have already paid for. Recently, for example, when developing a training course for supervisors of a manufacturing company, I was able to translate specific examples of how diversity of gender, race, or type of job was affecting employment experiences in the organization into several short cases. These cases were then analyzed in facilitated discussions with an experienced trainer. The supervisors gave their thoughts on how the situation might have been handled differently to produce a more effective result. The facilitator then summarized what had been said, giving her thoughts about points that the trainee group had missed. Because the raw material for the cases was taken from prior work with the organization, it saved the developmental cost that would otherwise have been incurred.

Another way to use research data to enhance education efforts is to use the results of work from one organization to demonstrate the value of the change process to other organizations. For example, in sessions teaching the change process of this book, it is often helpful to show data of the type shown in

Chapter Two to give an idea of what we hope to accomplish by using the process.

A third way to use data to educate is to include some published research data to support points that you want to make in teaching about some aspect of the change agenda. For example, in a training segment dealing with the effects of group identity on performance appraisals, you might include a summary of some of the most pertinent research as part of the trainer presentation in the session. Such data should be presented in a brief and easy-to-understand format. Research shows, for instance, that age and race identities often affect how people are rated. It also shows that an employee's gender and race often affect assumptions their managers make about the cause (or attribution) of performance achievements.[1]

Knowing this is true can lead people to question and to examine their own behavior and assumptions when they complete performance appraisals. It can also increase their motivation to learn about related topics such as stereotyping.

■ Diagnosing the Climate for Diversity

No change effort will get far without some form of organizational diagnosis. A formal measurement of the current state is necessary, both to guide action planning and to set a baseline for assessing progress. Although a thorough discussion of organizational diagnosis methods is beyond the scope of this book, here I offer some principles for effectiveness based on work with dozens of organizations.

Measure the Right Things

Measurement is valuable only if it focuses on true indicators of success. To identify these it will be helpful to start with some kind of explicit, research-based, conceptualization of the components of work climate that determine an organization's capacity to welcome and use workforce diversity as a resource for better performance. For me, this looks something like Table 4.1.

The items of Table 4.1 are based on empirical research on important organizational dynamics that are highly relevant to workforce diversity.[2] Even though all items are important, it is not necessary to include all fourteen in order to have a useable diagnosis of the organization climate. In selecting items to include, one criterion is "ease of measurement." In this regard, capturing some items, such as numbers 9 and 12, is very straightforward; for others, such as 11 and 14, it is much more complicated.

Unless you are thoughtful and insightful about the factors that define the climate for diversity, you are likely to miss key components. For example, consider the item labeled "mode of acculturation" in Table 4.1. The term *acculturation* refers to the way cultural differences are handled when parties from different cultural traditions are merged into one group. It applies to multiple types of group identifications, including gender, national origin, race, and organizational identity. The possibilities for acculturation mode include separation, with each party retaining its own identity and making little movement toward the work norms, values, and beliefs of the other. A second form is *assimilation,* in which the norms, values, and beliefs of the stronger, more dominant party or group are imposed on the other, less powerful party. Still another form is *pluralism,* in which each party is open to movement toward the culture of the other, the best traditions of each culture are carefully considered for adoption by the total enterprise, and each party retains some of their identity with the premerger culture.

The mode of acculturation in organizations in which acquisitions and joint ventures are prominent in the business strategy will have a great effect on the ability to integrate the workforces of the combining units and get them working together with maximum effectiveness as members of a newly defined "team." Yet

Table 4.1. Components of Diversity Climate

Individual-Level Measures	Definition
1. Amount of identity-group prejudice	Predisposition to dislike or have a negative attitude toward someone
2. Amount of stereotyping	Assuming that individuals have limited abilities or negative traits based on membership in a group
3. Amount of ethnocentrism	Preference for members of one's own "in-group"
4. Diversity-relevant personality traits	Examples: tolerance for ambiguity; authoritarian personality
5. Level of intergroup conflict	Conflict that is explicitly related to social-cultural group differences
6. Group identity strength	The extent to which a person feels a strong bond with his or her group
7. Quality of intergroup communication	Frequency and effectiveness of communications across groups
8. Cultural differences and similarities	Amount of cultural distance vs. overlap between cultures of groups
Organization-Level Measures	
9. Identity profile of workforce	Demographics of key differences in a defined work group or organization
10. Mode of acculturation	Method of handling cultural differences (assimilation vs. pluralism)
11. Content of organization culture	Key norms, values, beliefs
12. Power distribution among groups	Extent to which people of different identity groups have authority or power
13. People management practices and policies	Recruiting, promotions, compensation, physical work environment, member development, work schedules
14. Openness of informal networks	Extent to which people of all identity groups have access to social and communication networks

without an insightful model of what to study in diversity climate assessments, this aspect of the climate is easily omitted.

This example makes the point that we must marry content expertise with data collection savvy in order to get the best results when diagnosing a work climate with respect to a specific aspect of organizations, such as diversity. This is another place where many organizations will need help from external consultants.

Calibrate Carefully

Gathering data is helpful only if the data can be calibrated as good or bad in terms that make sense to the decision maker. Because there are few absolute standards of excellence in the area of organizational climate for people, calibration often requires some sort of comparison. There are three basic approaches to this. The first is the method, recently becoming popular, of external benchmarking against organizations that are known to be world class on the dimension of interest. In the diversity area, this means trying to compare to companies like Xerox, DuPont, U.S. West, AT&T, Corning, and others that have been consistently identified as world leaders on climate for diversity. This method of calibration has its advantages, but in my experience it is extremely difficult to find the full spectrum of data needed for organizations that are truly comparable to one's own. For example, it may be possible to get data on the gender breakdown of hires for a comparison company. But what about other gender climate factors, like levels of sexual harassment or of job stereotyping of women? Even if one has access to survey and other types of data, it may not be appropriate to use these data for comparison purposes because of differences in samples or in the context of data collection. For example, the degree to which "climate" survey data are positive is greatly influenced by factors such as the proportion of jobs that are salaried versus hourly, the national culture of the unit from which the data are taken, and whether or not there have been recent layoffs, bonuses, or other special events that tend to spike survey responses. For these reasons, external benchmarking has serious limitations as a calibration device.

An alternative is to calibrate by "internal benchmarking." This technique involves generating a database for units of one's own organization that is large enough to make cross-unit comparisons. For example, if there are a dozen accounting groups in your firm, you can get a good idea of performance levels by comparing each unit to the range and average of the set of twelve. This method does not avoid the problems of external benchmarking entirely but, in most cases, it will significantly reduce them.

A third method of calibration is to compare data for the same work unit at different times. This simply involves setting a measurement baseline and then evaluating performance based on changes over time.

The three methods just discussed can be combined. For instance, you might compare the percentage increase over a baseline in the first year of work to what has been achieved in a similar organization that is ahead of yours in applying the change process.

Triangulate Methods

Here I borrow the term *triangulation* from academia as a way to express the power of data drawn from multiple sources. Specifically, I recommend using a combination of interview data, survey data, data from the firm's computer information system, and direct observations. The inclusion of interview data offers a number of important benefits for work in this area. One such benefit is the ability to clarify the meaning of the questions being asked so that all respondents have the same understanding of them. A second benefit is the ability to probe and get further depth of information. For example, in addition to knowing that 60 percent of all employees see a problem with interdepartmental cooperation and communications, you can follow up to determine employees' ideas as to the cause of these difficulties. A third advantage of interview data is that they provide for an exchange of information. For example, the interviewer can use this opportunity to further educate the interviewee on the purpose of the change effort.

■ Measuring Progress

An old adage in business firms is that you get what you measure. To be sure, organizations need a formal plan of measurement for any major change effort. What kind of data should be used to measure progress on diversity efforts? A variety of metrics have been used, including those shown in Table 4.2.

A combination of several different types of metrics is advisable, but all must be selected to fit your organizational circumstances. For many measures, it will be helpful to look at both overall data and data sorted by identity groups. For example, rates of harassment are often two to three times higher for women in male-dominant organizations than they are for men. Likewise, turnover rates often differ significantly for various

Table 4.2. Examples of Metrics for Measuring Progress

Employee turnover

Employee absenteeism

Structured employee feedback (interview or survey data)

Levels of change in diversity profiles

Percent implementation of action plans

Positive job-offer-response ratio

Levels of identity-group-related complaints or litigation costs

Successful accommodations for persons with disabilities

identity groups such as gender, race, and type of job. In one recent case, an organization found that overall turnover rates were
modest, but the rate for engineers was much higher. This same
organization had acquired another firm several years earlier, and
in the period of time since then, turnover rates for former members of the acquired firm were significantly higher than those for
members of the acquiring organization. Distinctions like these,
which are important for managing diversity, are lost if only ag-
gregate data are used in measurement.

Lessons Learned About Measuring Progress

My experiences with measuring progress have led to several tips
for success that I want to share with you. These are presented next.

Communicate, Communicate, Communicate
When measuring progress, it is vitally important to have a consistently effective communications plan that keeps people ap-
prised of action steps and the results achieved. Further, when
the change effort is using feedback from the workforce (which
all change efforts should), the communications must help them
make connections between their feedback and the action steps.

The importance of communications about progress is illustrated by the following anecdote. Recently, during the work on
diversity in one of Alcoa's business units, I was talking with a
group of hourly employees about the need for further work to
manage diversity dynamics in their organization. Someone in
the group responded that supervisors needed to be trained on
diversity issues in order for work with hourly members to have
any lasting effect. When I explained that all supervisors in the
organization had just completed sixteen hours of diversity education within the last six months, the audience was stunned. Despite an active change effort in the organization for months
following a climate assessment, none of the thirty-five or so

people in the meeting seemed to know that this training had taken place.

The lesson to be learned is to stop just short of complete overkill when it comes to communications related to the change effort. This is important for other reasons, but it will also help make your measurement plan more effective.

Pay Attention to the Unit of Analysis

A second lesson learned in the measurement area concerns the relationship between measurement options and the unit of analysis for measurement. I have found that this relationship is shaped like the one in Figure 4.1.

To illustrate what Figure 4.1 shows, consider a mid-sized manufacturing firm of three thousand employees spread over seven different geographic locations across three countries. At the individual level, measurement options are constrained by the lack of responsibility for individuals over certain metrics. For example, it is appropriate to hold heads of departments responsible for employee turnover rates within that department, but it would certainly not be appropriate to measure nonsupervisory personnel on this item. At the other end of the spectrum, some

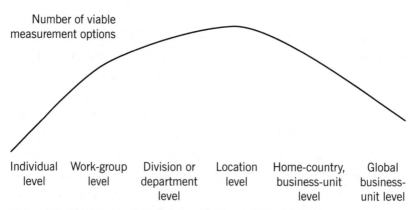

Figure 4.1. Relationship of Measurement Options to Unit of Analysis

metrics that are suitable at the location or home-country corpo-rate level may not be appropriate for use in other parts of the world. An example is measures of racial demographics. In be-tween these extremes, more options are available. The main point is that the number and type of metrics will be based partly on the level of analysis that we want to measure.

Set Appropriate Measurement Intervals
One final insight concerns determining the right intervals for measuring progress. Here the desire of change agents for short-term feedback must be balanced against what is prudent, given certain realities in the nature of the work being measured. For example, in a conversation I had with the head of a manufac-turing plant that had recently started to use the change process described in this book, the manager asked what measures he could use on a quarterly basis to assess how the plant was doing. My reply, while offering some ideas for short-term meas-urement, emphasized several points to keep in mind when set-ting measurement intervals:

- This kind of change doesn't happen overnight. The expecta-tions for movement within a quarter of a year should be very modest and should not be applied at all to some meas-ures (for example, the content of the organizational culture).
- Measurement intervals must be keyed closely to rates of ac-tion implementation. Too often there has not been enough real work done to warrant any reasonable expectation of measurable progress.
- Excessive frequency of measurement, especially where em-ployee feedback is used, can sour people on the change ef-fort and become a hindrance to change.
- The appropriateness of some metrics for use at short in-tervals (less than a year) will depend on the organization's specific circumstances. For example, looking at the gender

demographics of hiring or promotions on a quarterly basis may be appropriate in growth businesses or businesses with very high turnover rates but will not in other circumstances.

■ Some Caveats on Using Research

As the examples in this chapter suggest, research data can be a powerful tool in support of a change process focused on diversity. The use of data can backfire, however, if the credibility of the consultant or the internal sponsors of the change effort are damaged by missteps in the use of data. To this end, the following tips are suggested.

First, don't oversell the data. Err on the side of modesty in citing data to support conclusions. When the claims of change agents overshoot what a careful person would consider to be the boundary of the available data, the change advocates lose some legitimacy.

Second, make sure the people presenting the data have a deep understanding of the data and how they were collected. When data are presented that are not flattering to the organization, they will normally be challenged. Was the sample size large enough? Are differences statistically significant? How were interview participants selected? How do these data compare to those of other organizations? Nothing undermines a research effort in change work quicker than the inability to satisfy inquiring minds on questions such as these. I believe that a certain amount of testing the data is appropriate and necessary, so make sure presenters are prepared and do not come off as being defensive or have to respond repeatedly to questions by saying, "I don't know."

A third tip is to make sure the presentation of the data is user-friendly. A good rule of thumb is that if the average high school student doesn't understand a graphic, it probably needs to be revised. A related point is to avoid overloading people with data. Carefully select enough examples to make your point, but don't overwhelm people. When it comes to the main body of both written and oral reports of research, there is such a thing as too much data.

A fourth tip is to help your audience by making clear what *you* think the data mean. Of course, there are many possible interpretations of data, and people may not agree with yours, but you owe it to them to provide a starting point for making sense of the data. A good technique in this regard is to summarize with a short list of conclusions mapped to specific data points. This mapping does not have to be presented formally, but, at a minimum, the presenter should be prepared to explain precisely how the data and the conclusions are linked.

A final tip may seem obvious but is simply too important to omit: take every precaution to ensure the accuracy of the data. This means that any number that looks funny should be double-checked *before* it is presented to anyone. A related suggestion is to readily volunteer to check out any data the audience thinks are wrong. Explain the source of the data, but don't assume that everything you have to present is flawless. When we become defensive about our data, we begin to lose some influence with those we are trying to get committed to the cause.

CHAPTER SUMMARY

A major objective of this chapter has been to show that there is great value in research and measurement and that they are fundamental to the process of change for managing diversity. Using data to drive change means using data to increase commitment, enhance training, diagnose the climate for diversity, and measure progress.

Another message delivered in this chapter is that the term *data* should be defined broadly to include such things as survey feedback and even quotations showing how individual employees are thinking and feeling about their experiences at work. When drawn from a variety of sources and methods and used properly, the use of data can be a powerful force for organizational change.

Questions for Further Learning and Development

1. Of the four uses of data mentioned in the introduction to the chapter, which applications have been made in your organization?

2. Which of the items in the menu of diversity metrics shown in Table 4.2 are represented in the measurement plan for diversity in your organization? If no measurement plan exists, which of these factors do you believe should be included in the measurement plan for your organization?

3. How adequate is the CIS of your organization to provide the data needed to manage diversity effectively?

    Use the ideas for measures present in the chapter to make an assessment. Develop a list of items needed, if appropriate, adding to those mentioned in the chapter to reflect key interests for your situation. For example, in some organizations the number of languages spoken is a critical piece of data, but in others it is not.

    For any of the listed items not currently available, why have they been omitted?

    Should these omissions be corrected? (*Note:* the answer to this is not obvious because there are sometimes good business reasons for omitting certain items from a computer information system [CIS], even though having the data would be helpful.)

4. Most organizations have some kind of employee feedback process at periodic intervals. For example, many do annual employee surveys. If your organization has such a survey or something similar, evaluate it using the diversity climate factors shown in Table 4.1. To what extent are these diversity factors captured in your existing employee feedback process?

    If the current research mechanisms are inadequate, how should this be rectified?

Create Effective Education

The need for education is well established as a staple of organization change—and no less so for change related to diversity. Unfortunately, much of the work that has taken place to date under the label of "diversity training" has failed to produce any lasting impact. For example, a study by Sara Rynes and Ben Rosen of more than seven hundred organizations shows that only about one-third of diversity training efforts are viewed as creating lasting results in the company using them.[1]

Why is this the case? In this chapter I discuss some of the pitfalls of designing and delivering education on diversity and offer some tips for improving the return on investment on diversity training. My approach is to interweave the two topics of *pitfalls to avoid* and *best practices to imitate* for each of the main ingredients of training: content, format and logistics, participants, and facilitation.

■ Content

What is the critical content for education on diversity? This is a multidimensional question. One dimension is the specification of the required subtopics; another is the linkage among the topics; a third is the type of content. For example, is the content focused on individuals, on organizations, or both? Or does the content attend to understanding the effects of diversity, to how to respond to diversity, to attracting diversity—or to all of these?

Critical Subtopics

Addressing the issue of subtopics is greatly facilitated by the careful articulation of a conceptual model that defines your view of the important dynamics of diversity—your theory of diversity, so to speak. The need for such a theory has been a recurring theme of this book. Figure 5.1 shows how the components of diversity climate that were shown in Table 4.1 can be configured into a conceptual framework. This framework can then be used for guidance in designing diversity education. For example, using the theory of diversity effects shown in Figure 5.1, the training curriculum shown in Table 5.1 was created for the education of change leaders in the work with Alcoa.

You will notice the close correspondence of topic areas between the training outline and the conceptual model of diversity effects, as recorded in Figure 5.1. This correspondence has several advantages. First, it increases the chances that the most important empirically based topics will receive attention in the education effort. Second, it provides a means of linking the top-

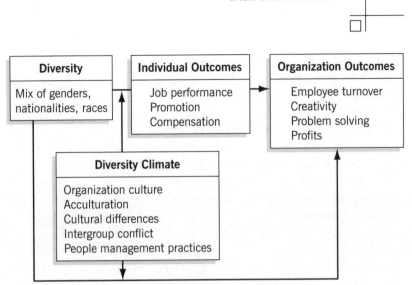

Figure 5.1. Theory of Diversity Effects

Source: Adapted from Figure 1.1 of *Cultural Diversity in Organizations Theory, Research & Practice* by Taylor Cox Jr., 1993. Berrett Koehler Publishing. Items listed in each box are exemplary, not exhaustive.

ics together in a way that gives coherence to the training. Often such training is experienced as simply a collection of seemingly unrelated learning events. Third, it ensures that certain key messages, such as the connection between diversity competency and organizational performance, get reinforced throughout the change process.

The curriculum shown in Table 5.1 was initially used for training members of the corporate diversity steering committee of Alcoa. It has subsequently been used as the core content of leader education in many of the Alcoa business units, including many training events in which union leaders and management people have been trained together. Incidentally, some of the most significant breakthroughs toward changing the culture of the company occurred in these combined union-management leadership sessions. Also notice that the curriculum has a modular design. This provides greater flexibility of delivery formats. For example, modules 7 and 8 are typically used in all-manager groups.

Table 5.1. Developing Competency to Manage Diversity:
A Curriculum for Leaders

1. The meaning and importance of diversity
   - Definitions of key terms
   - Linkage of diversity to organization performance
2. Diversity and organization culture
   - Norms of a culture that is diversity-supportive or diversity-toxic
   - Diagnosing your organization
   - A process for changing organizational culture
3. Cultural differences
   - Examples of cultural differences
4. Acculturation
   - Modes of acculturation and implications for diversity
   - Cultural distance and the burden of conformity
5. Issues of affirmative action
   - Defining affirmative action (toward a shared understanding)
   - The concerns of "reverse" discrimination
   - Characteristics of effective affirmative action programs
6. Prejudice, stereotyping, and intergroup conflict
   - Definition of terms
   - Behavioral manifestations of stereotyping and prejudice
7. Group identity effects in hiring, promotion, and performance appraisal
   - Ways in which these management processes are influenced by social-cultural identity factors such as gender and national origin, as well as ways to minimize these effects
8. Institutionalizing diversity competency
   - Assessment tools for individuals and organizations
   - Next steps for extending learning and development

Customizing the Content

Canned training programs should be avoided in favor of training that is customized to fit your organization. One application of this idea is that the content be well matched to your learning objectives. For example, the main objective of the curriculum shown in Table 5.1 is to deepen the knowledge of the participants concerning the phenomenon of diversity so that they can lead change with a better understanding. Given this objective, the process for changing organizations receives only passing attention. When the objective is to help people learn to respond to the challenges of diversity, the change process, which forms the outline of this book, would be much more heavily emphasized.

Another point on content customization is to tailor the topics to fit the diversity dimensions that are most salient in your organization. In some cases, this means identity-specific content. For example, Ford Motor Company developed a training curriculum that started with an overview of the topic of diversity for all employees and then moved to modules on specific types of identity such as "gender" and "persons with disabilities." The modular design allowed segments of the organization to focus their training investment on dimensions of difference that seemed most relevant.

I want to emphasize that the content need not be planned around specific identity groups in order to provide for some customization for differences in salient identity groups. Another approach is to use a phenomena-based curriculum. This approach would be similar to the one specified in Table 5.1 but with different examples in different organizations. For example, when discussing acculturation issues in one organization, the identity of race might be used; gender might be used in another. In still another, the focus might be on what happens when two organizations are merged. In each case, the participant is learning similar concepts, such as cultural distance, cultural overlap, differential burdens of conformity, and so on, but the vehicle for elaborating these concepts is different and more socially relevant. The relevance of content is also facilitated by using examples from the climate assessment of the organization, as explained in Chapter Four.

A final point about content customization concerns the stage of the learning process that is to be addressed. Again, the objective of the training is key. Based on our experience training thousands of people, my colleagues in my consulting group and

I find that people progress through three stages of learning: awareness, deeper knowledge, and behavioral change. If the objective of the training is to raise awareness, this is facilitated by content that requires the participant to be self-reflective and to hear about the experiences and interpretations of others. If the objective is to deepen knowledge, giving the person some new information about the subject (for example, a short summary of research on the subject at hand) is often helpful. If the objective is to change behavior, then the training must require participants to think about action steps for translating new insights into doing something differently as they perform their jobs.

Obviously, there is room for overlap among these stages of learning within single training events, but we find that one of the greatest causes of failure (or perceived failure) of diversity training is that the content and learning objectives are not well matched, or participants and training designers do not have the same expectations of the training objectives. A common scenario is when participants come to a training session expecting the training to teach behaviors (stage 3), when the session is actually designed to provide awareness (stage 1 of the learning process).

Fixing the problem of incongruence between objectives and content is not simply a matter of better design or communications, although both are important. It is also a matter of aligning the training objectives with a variety of other factors, such as the stage of the participant's development, the time available to deliver the education, and the skill level of the facilitator. Some of these issues will be addressed further in the next section.

■ Format and Logistics

The format and logistics aspect of diversity education takes in such things as the time and method of instruction. I cannot provide a comprehensive discussion of these issues but will hit some of the main points I have learned about how to make this type of training more effective.

Time

A major reason for lost effectiveness with diversity training is failure to provide sufficient time to accommodate the training objectives and training situation. Naturally the "right" amount of time is a function of many things. One of the most important is the learning stage or stages to be addressed. If the objective is to go beyond awareness, significantly more time must be planned. This need not mean longer training events, but it does mean a commitment to higher levels of total training hours spread over some reasonable period of time. An ubiquitous error is to plan a one-day training event with the objective, expressed or implied, of bringing people through all three stages of the learning model (awareness, deeper knowledge, and behavior change). Whenever we allow a training event, for any reason, to go off with this kind of expectation, we are doomed to failure before we start.

A more reasonable approach is to plan sequenced events, each deepening the participants' level of competency, for example, a series of three days of education where the weight of the content shifts throughout the sequence as shown in Figure 5.2.

This example, which is based on roughly eight hours for each stage of the learning process, should be viewed as a bare *minimum* specification and not necessarily as the ideal time commitment.

Another factor affecting the amount of time needed to do effective training on diversity is the level of participant response desired, that is, whether you are trying to foster learning at an intellectual (cognitive) level, an emotional level, or a spiritual level. Each of these represents successively deeper levels of learning and accordingly will take more time to reach and fulfill. For example, here is a common scenario of training that I

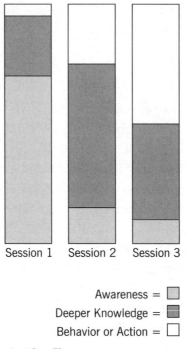

Session 1   Session 2   Session 3

Awareness =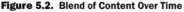
Deeper Knowledge = ▣
Behavior or Action = ☐

Figure 5.2. Blend of Content Over Time

believe is relatively ineffective in the long term. The facilitator is successful in getting a number of participants to tell stories about times when they were deeply hurt by insensitive behavior related to a group identity such as gender, national origin, or race. Many members of the group are emotionally affected by these poignant testimonials, and there is a strong buzz about these events during and immediately following the training. Unfortunately, the time it takes to produce these magic moments consumes virtually all of the limited time set aside for the training, leaving the participants on their own to bring closure to the raw emotions that have been exposed and to decipher the meaning of the stories for their future behavior. The result is that although this training often gets high marks in participant evaluations taken during the training, it often does not produce lasting change in the organization.

Although this scenario is all too familiar among veterans of diversity education, the fact that it occurs in part because of a failure to plan training time properly is often missed. The upshot of my message is that the time allocated is often insufficient to achieve the training objectives and that the matching of time and objectives is complex. The examples I have mentioned are only two of the most important ways in which the correspondence of time and objectives must be analyzed.

Method of Instruction

The method or format of instruction takes in such things as the amount of lecture versus participant interaction and the vehicles of learning. I will comment briefly on each of these.

Lecture Versus Interaction
One hears a lot today about the need to use "adult learning" techniques when training in organizations. A prominent feature of adult learning is to minimize the use of lecture and maximize the use of discussion among participants. This insight has led to the extensive use of small-group discussions in training. For diversity training these discussions are invaluable, as they provide opportunities for the participants to hear, firsthand, how people of other social and cultural backgrounds think and feel differently than they do.

Although there is no question about the value of participant interaction in diversity education, I believe that the time spent in training will not be maximized unless it includes at least a few significant segments of lecture by facilitators who have a deep understanding of the topic. This will provide for the much-needed transfer of knowledge from the expert who is conducting the training to the people who are trainees. Too often this transfer of knowledge does not occur, and although participants get insight and enjoyment from hearing how their peers think and feel about the issues under discussion, they do not get enough guidance about how they *should* think about the issues. This is what my colleague Noel Tichy calls "the teachable point of view." There is a point of view to be taught on many of the issues raised in diversity discussions, and the facilitator has an obligation to get this across.

I am not suggesting that the segments of lecture be lengthy; a few short ones is best. One approach is to sandwich the lectures around an interactive event. This involves kicking off the subtopic with a fifteen- to twenty-minute lecture that provides some background information or concepts to be used in the interactive activity. Then, after the interactive activity, come back to a short, perhaps ten-minute lecture to provide the facilitator's perspective on what the participants should have learned and to tie this part of the training to the content that has gone before.

The amount of lecture should be adjusted to training context factors. For example more lecture time is needed when participants have had little previous exposure to diversity education and when the focus of the education is on the first two stages of the learning process (awareness and deeper knowledge).

Vehicles of Learning
Like other forms of training, diversity education benefits from the use of a variety of learning vehicles such as films, case analyses, role plays, and small-group discussions. All of these tools are useful, but each can also be ineffective if overused. A common mistake, for example, is to show too many videos.

Some excellent videos are available to help teach about diversity. Some that I have found effective include

A Class Divided (Jane Elliot's workshop on prejudice; available from WGBH Educational Foundation of PBS, Alexandria, Virginia)

May the Best Man Win (depicts the gender case of the glass ceiling; available from MTI Film and Video, Northbrook, Illinois)

Productivity and the Self Fulfilling Prophecy (teaches the critical concept of the SFP, which is highly relevant to diversity; available from CRM Films, Carlsbad, California)

The Encouraging Manager (management style video that can be easily linked to diversity; available from Star Thrower Distribution, St. Paul, Minnesota)

Going International (depicts differences of national culture that, though overstated, are relevant; available from Griggs, Inc., San Francisco)

The Color of Fear (filmed focus group of people talking about race issues in the United States; available from Stir Fry Productions, Oakland, California)

Here are some tips for using videos:

- Use short ones—fifteen minutes or less when possible; use excerpts from longer videos.
- Ask the participants to watch for specific things as they watch and to write things down.
- Facilitators should have a list of the important learning points from the film.

Case analyses can also be effective tools for learning about diversity.[2] They are especially useful for getting people into the action stage of learning because participants must decide on a response to a specific situation. Here are a few tips for using cases:

- Use short cases (one or two pages). Longer cases should only be used if they can be read in advance.

- Where possible, develop some cases from the organization's own data (for example, based on feedback from a recent climate assessment).
- Ask participants to determine a response to the case individually before addressing it in a group.
- Make sure the facilitator communicates a point of view about effective response to the case to be shared during the case discussion.

Role plays can also be effective for learning about diversity. Indeed, there are organizations that provide professional dramatic actors to teach about diversity.[3] I have seen professional drama used in this way, and it is usually very well received. Of course, role plays can also be designed and played by the participants themselves, and this has the advantage of getting people directly involved in practicing new behaviors.

I have had mixed success with using participant role plays. They can fall flat if the learning messages are not clearly defined through discussion of scenes that are acted out. Another risk is that this type of education, especially the use of professional dramatic actors, is entertaining but leaves no lasting impact of new knowledge. Here are a few tips for avoiding these pitfalls:

- Make sure to give the participants help in interpreting what they have seen acted out.
- Make an explicit tie between the acting and the theory of diversity on which the training is based.
- Coach participants but don't over-script them; allow for some spontaneity and personality.

Another vehicle for learning is small-group discussions. This device is nearly always used in training and is especially important for learning about diversity because insight into how others are thinking and perceiving things is a major part of diversity education. Consider the following suggestions for using small-group discussions to teach about diversity:

- To the extent possible, create diversity in the discussion groups on the dimensions of diversity that are most directly addressed in the activity.
- Don't overuse these discussions (two or three in an eight-hour training session is usually enough).
- Create a way for the small groups to hear some of what was discussed in other groups.
- Explicitly tie outcomes of the discussions back to the session objectives and theory of diversity on which the training was based.

■ Participants

Several key, interrelated issues pertain to the participants in diversity education. These include how large the groups should be, the scope of job types and levels to be covered, the mix of participants in individual training sessions, and the selection and preparation of participants. Each of these will be briefly addressed.

Group Size

Over the years, a sort of industry norm has emerged that diversity training classes should be in the range of fifteen to twenty-five people. Taking into account the need for organizations to make every reasonable effort to save costs, we typically use twenty-five for planning purposes. There are, however, contingencies that affect this to some degree. Recently, I led a group of upper-middle managers of Alcoa in a three-hour session on diversity with the following objectives:

- Briefing on data from the change project
- Comments on requirements of leading diversity change efforts
- Assessment of diversity-supportive behaviors

Because this content could be effectively handled in a format of presentations with brief discussion, a rather large group of about thirty-seven people could be accommodated. On another occasion, I led a group of about one hundred people from the sales and marketing organization of the Buick Motors Division of General Motors in a two-hour diversity education experience where the objective was simply to understand business reasons for investing in diversity change work. Because the objective was very clear and very narrow, and because it lent itself to one-way communication from an "expert" presenter, this session was highly effective with the large group.

However, in many situations maintaining a smaller-size group is crucial to meeting the learning objectives. For example, a client recently asked a trainer from my consulting organization whether a two-day session planned for twenty-five people to prepare them to function as leaders of diversity change efforts could be expanded to accommodate sixty-five people! Our response was a resounding "No way!" Fortunately, the client saw our point and agreed to split the group into two sessions. Cost pressures notwithstanding, nothing is gained by running people through an education event in which a major part of the learning is lost because of the inability to have sufficient dialogue between the facilitator and participants and among the participants themselves. When planners continue to push for large group size after hearing the reasons that it is unwise, I become suspicious that they are not serious about learning but rather view diversity education as simply a do-it-quick, check-it-off-and-move-on activity. This kind of training is a waste of money.

Scope and Mix

Scope in this context refers to the breadth of job types and organizational levels to be covered by the diversity education. For example, it is customary to have all employees participate in basic diversity awareness education, but organizations sometimes limit participation to salaried members or even to people in managerial jobs. A basic question for organizations with large numbers of unionized employees is whether or not to include hourly members in planned diversity education events. This decision is sometimes complicated by the desire to make participation in the training mandatory. I have found that unions often prefer strongly that training of this type be voluntary.

Mix refers to the level of variety in types of jobs and organizational levels that are represented in any one session of training. Here the standard practice is to maximize variety within groups.

The impact of decisions about scope and mix on the cost of the education is usually straightforward, but less well understood is the impact of these decisions on the execution of the training itself. For example, the mixing of hourly and management people in training groups adds richness to the composition of the group, but it also makes the facilitator's job a lot tougher. What should be done with topics normally covered that are not highly relevant to the hourly workforce? How do you keep people focused on the issues at hand and out of extraneous issues like wage fairness? How do you create openness and candor when there may be a high level of distrust or conflict in the history of relationships between unions that represent some hourly workers and the management?

We have found that, in most cases, the downside of having to respond to these new challenges is outweighed by the potential benefits, but adjustments do have to be made. Two examples will illustrate these points. In one case the downside of high scope and mix and the need to make adjustments to accommodate them was demonstrated in a training event designed to include "type of job" as one of the diversity dimensions to be explicitly addressed in the training. Although there was plenty of evidence that stereotyping, prejudice, and other diversity dynamics were affecting the ability of hourly and management members to work well together, the facilitators were unable, despite the most heroic efforts, to keep the group focused on these issues. Instead the sessions routinely degenerated into preoccupation with contractual labor relations—so much so that we had to reluctantly pull the content on job-type diversity out of the training altogether in order to get the education back on track.

In another case the benefits of the inclusion of hourly and management members together in the same training events were demonstrated during a two-day education event planned to prepare leaders of diversity change work. The organization was unionized, and leaders of both the local union and the local management met together. A major breakthrough in the education occurred when one of the union leaders challenged the other union leaders present with the question: "Do you believe that there is equal opportunity for women to be elected to the highest offices within our union?" This person then proceeded to give his answer to the question—an emphatic "No." The matter under discussion at the time was the extent to which the issues being addressed in the training were really union issues or just "company" issues. This was one of several breakthrough events that occurred during this two-day training. The aftermath was increasing common leadership of the union and management for the work on diversity in that organization.

Before leaving this segment, I should mention that another connotation of participant mix that deserves careful attention is the demographic profile of the group on dimensions of diversity that are relevant to the training objectives. For example, learning about gender diversity is greatly facilitated by having a reasonable balance of men and women in participant groups. This, of course, is not always possible. When the current work population is too highly skewed to achieve identity balance in training sessions, my advice is to plan as many balanced groups as possible and then have some same-identity groups. This approach accomplishes several things. First, it solves the basic problem that there simply aren't enough members of some social-cultural group to go around. Second, it ensures that at least some groups will have *genuine* diversity on the dimension in question. The fact is that having a large number of groups with "gender diversity" defined as one or two women in a group of twenty-five people is *not* better than having a smaller number of groups where the gender mix is no worse than two-thirds men and one-third women, combined with a number of all-male groups. The exception is when the two or three available women are especially courageous, in tune with the relevant issues, and motivated to maximize their contributions to the training discussions. Third, this approach creates an opportunity in the same-identity groups (for example, all-male groups) for some unusually frank and focused discussions about the issues from the point of view of the majority group.

Selection and Preparation of Participants

Ordinarily, participants for training should be randomly selected within designated work populations, but there are at least two important exceptions. First, as just mentioned, it is sometimes necessary to over-sample from specific identity groups to create diversity on dimensions of interest. Second, it is often wise to seed some of the early sessions with handpicked people who will maximize the probability of achieving the learning objectives. Important criteria for picking such people include knowledge of the diversity issues in your workplace *and* willingness to speak out in a mixed group of work colleagues. By doing this, the all-important word-of-mouth publicity from the first few training sessions can be leveraged to build a positive "point-of-entry" mind-set for people coming for training.

Hand picking early participants is only one useful idea for creating the right point-of-entry mind-set. Another is to use pre-education events. The purpose of these events is to promote accurate and positive expectations about what the training will be like. One example of such events comes from my work at Exxon's Research and Engineering Company. When the first diversity education session was held there in the early 1990s, I sat in as an observer. The session was a disaster. People did not really open up and discuss honestly the issues at hand, even though I heard people talking in the hallways during breaks and knew that they were aware of diversity issues in the organization. At the close of the session, one of the facilitators made the mistake of asking for everyone to verbalize his or her reaction to the training. This led to a series of mostly negative comments being offered, which spiraled downward as they progressed from person to person until the room began to feel like a funeral parlor. Afterward, when we were debriefing what went wrong, I made the observation that the bad outcome was not necessarily a function of the content or the manner of facilitation. Rather, the problem was that the participants came in with expectations that were (1) widely different and (2) inconsistent with the objectives of the training. One major disconnect was that a lot of people did not understand that the goal was simply to begin to raise awareness. Another disconnect was that the participants did not understand the extent to which the learning would depend on their willingness to share *their own thoughts and experiences* relating to the topic versus getting information from the facilitators.

To address these concerns, the company planned short pre-workshop meetings for all training participants. At these meetings, the people selected for the upcoming training sessions were briefed on the purpose of the training, on what to expect, and on what they should be prepared to bring to the table for the training to be a success. Questions were answered, and an attempt was made to get people more comfortable with the training before they actually participated in it. Although this is admittedly a somewhat costly solution, we found that it can make a big difference to the success level of the training.

One final idea for participant preparation is the use of pre-work. For example, it often helps to have participants read one or two articles or a book relating to diversity before attending training. This is especially effective when the person who designed or is delivering the training wrote the material being used. Advance reading gives participants some knowledge of the perspective of the training organization and also enhances their perception of the legitimacy and expertise of the trainers.

Other forms of pre-work that are sometimes appropriate include having participants collect data from coworkers on their diversity-competency behaviors, read a case study, or have a discussion with a coworker about the diversity issues in their work unit. Regarding the former, I have developed a self-assessment tool that can be used to gather data on diversity-competency behaviors. The tool can be used by participants in training to assess themselves and then be compared with the feedback from coworkers as a reality check.[4]

Regardless of the type of pre-work used, the objective is to enhance participants' readiness to think and learn about the ways diversity affects behavior and performance at work and to increase their motivation to learn about the subject. Although I have found that steps such as the ones I have described are very helpful for preparing people to learn, and hence get better results, they are not standard practice in diversity education. Most people come to training sessions with little more preparation than a memo stating the topic, date, time, and place. Thus, more attention to participant preparation is one of the keys to more effective training on diversity.

■ Facilitation

The final main ingredient of education related to change initiatives is the facilitation of the learning. Many other sources provide general information on effective facilitation.[5] Here I will limit my comments to issues related to diversity education, including opening and closing the training, handling sensitive subject matter, and building internal expertise.

Opening and Closing the Training

Effective openings and closings of sessions are essential to success with training on any subject. They are especially crucial with diversity education, however, because so many participants arrive with a mind-set that is somewhere between skepticism about whether the training is worthwhile and open hostility. Skillful openings help break these barriers by establishing the place of the education on diversity within the context of the organization's business strategy. This context is often best provided by a high-level member of the organization rather than by outside consultants.

Many organizations try to accomplish this contextualization by using a video of the CEO talking about diversity and the reasons for its priority among business objectives. A video of this type can be helpful, but it is not nearly as effective as having a live human, whom the participants know, come to the session to present these ideas. A kick-off by a high-level local leader accomplishes several things, not the least of which is to signal that this work is, indeed, a high priority. The mere presence of a top manager or union leader makes a statement about the value and importance of the education. In addition, it affords an opportunity for people to see firsthand the leader's level of passion for the work on diversity. Assuming that it is high and that the leader has a reputation for personal integrity, the likelihood of the training being effective is increased significantly. At a recent one-day education event involving HR managers of a large company, the president of a large business unit of the company kicked the meeting off with an appeal for the focus and energy of the group on the issues to be discussed that day. Afterward, one of the participants stated to the group that he had come to the meeting somewhat skeptical about his involvement, but "when [the president] personally comes to a meeting like this and says that he needs my help to work on this issue, that really got my attention."

Closing training is also important, and more so with diversity education because so often the training leaves people feeling high and dry, with no clear direction on what to do next. A closing that establishes links back to the workplace will diminish this problem. One way to do this is through an activity in which people create a personal action plan for follow-up after the training. Additional likelihood of follow-up can be obtained by asking participants to create "accountability partners"—people who will meet with them periodically after the training to monitor and encourage them to make progress on their action agendas.

The participation of high-level line leaders at the close of training can also add impact. Recently, in one of the Alcoa business units, the entire team of four line-management heads attended the closing session of a two-day diversity training session for supervisors. They reiterated their personal support and commitment to the diversity change initiative and promised continuing action and communications to follow up on the training. They also took questions from the group. This was a very impressive and effective way to bring closure to two days of work on a topic whose importance, in the minds of some, was still a little suspect.

Handling Sensitive Subject Matter

Facilitators of diversity education must be skilled at dealing with issues that are (1) laden with emotion, such as experiences with prejudice and discrimination, (2) controversial, such as affirmative action, and (3) deeply personal, such as topics that touch on the spiritual life of participants. The necessary qualities go beyond strong facilitation and include empathy, the ability to maintain balance when dealing with controversy, the ability to foster trust and create a sense of safety for participants, and the willingness to do just the right amount of self-disclosure. For example, how many trainers in your organization feel confident enough to handle a training session in which a person announces for the first time in public a lesbian sexual orientation and makes it clear that the training will not be a success for her unless the dimension of sexual orientation is addressed directly? If, in the same session a confrontation develops between Christian and Jewish participants and gays and lesbians, how does one diffuse this situation? Both situations have happened to me, and I can tell you that they were not easy to handle.

Because diversity brings some special requirements in terms of facilitation, steps should be taken to prepare for them. First, select facilitators very carefully, keeping in mind the kinds of criteria just discussed. Second, give extra preparation to trainers, using what-if scenarios such as the two examples just mentioned involving sexual orientation. Third, facilitators should have some knowledge of intercultural differences, especially for the national-origin groups that are most prevalent in your work population. Fourth, it helps to use multiple trainers whenever possible. This doubles the probability of having a trainer who is prepared to handle any sensitive situation that may arise. It also helps in situations where the identity of the trainer may make it hard for her or him to provide the needed type of facilitation. For example, it often works better for the merits of affirmative action to be presented by a white male, especially if there is tension and conflict in the group about this tool. As another example, consider the situation mentioned earlier in the chapter in which the group of hourly and salaried participants could not get past labor contract issues in order to focus on diversity dynamics. The resolution of this situation would have been greatly facilitated by having a joint training team that included a member of the hourly workforce.

Unfortunately, most diversity training is carried out without the benefits of multiple trainers. In these cases, the importance of having a highly skilled person doing the training is even more apparent. This brings us to another decision of some magnitude—the matter of whether or not facilitators should be external or internal. Although there are pros and cons for both, the most central thing to be concerned about in making this decision is to have the necessary level of expertise. Consulting help is expensive and should be used only when there is a clear business necessity. However, given what has been said here about the teaching of diversity being uniquely difficult and the reality that many of today's organizations are very lean on professional facilitation talent, many firms will find that outside help is a must. Having said this, I strongly believe that the development of internal expertise to deliver diversity education is also a must. I say more about this point next.

Building Internal Expertise

My experience with change work on diversity suggests to me that unless you create layers of people in your organization with true expertise on the topic of diversity, the change effort will stall. What I mean by *layers* is that the knowledge base must go beyond one or two people in the HR department. For example, when diversity education was first developed in the Philips Display Components Division of Philips Electronics, we created training teams composed of one internal person and one external trainer. A cadre of carefully picked people from various functions and organizational levels were prepared with train-the-trainer sessions and then worked with my trainers to deliver training to their colleagues. As they gained experience, they took on more training responsibility. For this relatively small organization of around twenty-five hundred people, a group of ten well-prepared people would provide them ample back-up to ensure that the work would keep going, even if a few highly skilled people left the organization or were otherwise unavailable to continue as diversity resource people.

In another case an Alcoa plant with around twenty-five hundred people has trained a cadre of a dozen or so conflict-resolution facilitators. Some of these people serve with others on a diversity council, which maintains continuous learning on the subject of diversity and is therefore developing some depth of knowledge on the subject. The presence of these two groups, along with key people in the HR organization, gives this plant a critical mass of knowledgeable people who have been prepared to continue the work. After three years of working closely with a consultant, the organization is now well positioned to fly solo.

The creation of internal resources to carry out high-quality education on diversity issues is paramount for long-term success in organization change. This statement applies more or less generically for change work in organizations, but there is again something a bit special about diversity education. Unlike subjects like financial management, safety, production processes, and many others, there is rarely a group of people inside the organization who have depth of education on the general subject area of diversity. This means that most organizations are starting from zero to build knowledge of this area rather than refining an already established foundation of basic principles. *Thus there is a complex and increasingly well-developed base of knowledge on managing diversity, but there is probably no one in your organization who has been extensively trained on it.* This is an enormously important point for change leaders to understand and to keep in mind when doing work in this area. Given this fact, you should be prepared to make a significant investment in a group of people in order to establish adequate internal resources to keep the work alive and working well long after the consultants have gone.

CHAPTER SUMMARY

This chapter has addressed some of the most important things to keep in mind when developing and delivering education on the subject of diversity. The advice offered here is based on experiences with hundreds of training efforts involving thousands of participants. Despite the very lackluster record to date of sustained results from diversity training efforts, the use of education in this area as a major lever of change remains vital. Applying the ideas shared here about the content and format of the training, the selection and preparation of participants, and the creation of strong training facilitation should greatly increase the chances that your education interventions will be effective.

Nevertheless, I close with a caveat. Training, no matter how good it is, will not produce lasting change in your organization unless it is coupled with the elements of the process discussed in the other chapters of this book. Unfortunately, too many would-be change leaders give lip service to the concept of comprehensiveness in the change model but do not really follow through and apply it. The power of the process is in the application of all its facets working together.

Questions for Further Learning and Development

1. If you have participated in diversity training in the past, how effective was the training in terms of (1) impact at the time and (2) promoting long-term change?

Using the curriculum in Table 5.1, assess the breadth of topic coverage that has occurred in the training that you have received.

Combine the list in Table 5.1 with the three levels of learning shown in Figure 5.2. to create a matrix with the two dimensions "breadth of coverage" and "depth of coverage." Use this matrix to assess the effectiveness of any previous training. If you are planning to do diversity education, use the matrix from the previous step to think about the appropriate breadth and depth in your education plan.

2. Who in your organization is able and available to do training on diversity? If there is no one, who are the likely candidates to be developed for expertise on this topic? What can be done to establish a cadre of internal facilitators to do diversity training in your firm?

3. What are the earmarks of good facilitation for education on diversity?

Assume that you have been asked to serve as a facilitator for a training session on diversity. Putting aside the issue of learning the content, what special challenges do you foresee for doing the facilitation? What could you do to help prepare for these challenges?

Align Organizational Systems and Practices

One of the central messages of this book is that change to welcome and leverage diversity must be done in a systems approach, that is, with recognition of the organization as a social system with interdependent components. A major cause of disappointing results from past efforts on diversity has been the omission of the principles of systems theory. Organizations are social systems, and changing them requires that all major components of the system be reviewed and changed to achieve alignment—in this case, alignment with the presence of increasing diversity.

Three main categories of work climate must be examined when doing systems alignment work: *time, space,* and *people process. Time factors* have to do with the way time is scheduled for the performance of work. *Space factors* concern aspects of the physical work environment. *People process factors* are practices designed to manage the acquisition of human talent and their employment outcomes. These categories, along with a list of elements that make them up, are shown in Table 6.1.

Although a discussion of the implications of all of these factors is beyond the scope of this book, examples will be given here for five elements of Table 6.1 to illustrate how to do the work of system alignment. The five elements are (1) time-off policies, (2) the presence of class distinctions, (3) recruiting practices, (4) performance appraisal practices, and (5) career development practices.

Table 6.1. Climate Factors to Be Aligned with Diversity

Time Factors
- Length of the typical workday
- Days of work per week
- Use of overtime
- Time-off policies (vacation, leave, personal days)
- Retirement policies
- Level of work schedule flexibility

Space Factors
- Cleanliness of the workspace
- Extent to which physical barriers separate people at work
- Presence of class distinctions in specifications of physical spaces at work

People Process Factors
- Recruiting practices
- Promotion practices
- Compensation policies
- Performance appraisal practices
- Career development and succession planning practices

■ Time-Off Policies

Time-off policies specify the ability of employees to take paid and unpaid time off from work. It is not difficult to see the connection between such policies and the diversity in the workforce. Trends like the increasing presence of dual-career couples, increasing participation of women in the workforce (which is old news in the United States but still developing in many other countries of the world), the surging interest of men in parental activities,[1] and the rising desire to trade income for leisure time have piqued interest in policies on time off.

The most fundamental implication of these trends is that if your organization has more liberal time-off policies, you will be better able to attract, retain, and motivate the diverse workforce. This said, the connections between diversity and work-time policies have many subtleties, as illustrated by the following anecdote. Several years ago, I received a call from an employee of a small manufacturing plant. The employee was upset because her supervisor had denied her time off to attend her grandson's college graduation. She appealed to me for help because she knew I was working with her employer on a change process to become more welcoming of diversity. Of course, I explained that this was not the kind of thing that I could become directly involved in and advised her to talk to the local HR professional in her company. But some insights here deserved attention in the company's management of diversity effort, so I passed them on to the plant HR manager. The woman was African American. My familiarity with differences in life history for African Americans compared to Anglo-Americans immediately raised three concerns. First, there was a greater likelihood that the grandmother had a particularly close relationship with the grandson. This is because higher levels of poverty, having children at younger ages, and a higher incidence of young-age deaths often results in grandparents being more involved in childrearing for African American children. Second, because young adult Anglo-Americans are twice as likely as African Americans to complete college, there was a greater chance that this was a first-generation college graduation and therefore an especially momentous achievement in this family. Third, because African Americans have a long history of discrimination based on their race, there was a much greater likelihood that this woman, compared to her Anglo peers, would attribute the decision not to grant time off to her race. For all of these reasons, I knew there was likely to be some *extra* sensitivity toward the no-time-off policy. This is an example of how a policy, even if it is enforced the same for all employees (which this worker maintained was not the case), does not necessarily have the same impact on members of all social and cultural backgrounds in a work group.

Even though it is tempting to simply point out that you can improve the alignment of time-off policies with diversity by increasing the opportunity for employees in all job categories to get paid and unpaid time off, there are clearly some competing pressures that work against this solution. If your organization is like many that have reduced the ratio of number of employees to work performed as a way to improve productivity, pressures for the remaining workforce to work longer hours have risen. As a consequence of this it is difficult to grant time off as an accommodation to the requirements of diversity. This example reminds us that when aligning organizational policies and practices to any one aspect of the business strategy, we must always keep an eye on the big picture in order to arrive at the right decision for the overall business strategy. This is a function to be performed by top executives and represents another example of strategic integration, as discussed in Chapter Three.

■ Presence of Class Distinctions

A principle that is virtually universal in human systems is the tendency to organize social groups into status hierarchies. In most societies we find clearly identifiable status hierarchies of gender, socioeconomic class, work specialization, race, and so on. *In general, a work climate becomes more diversity friendly when it avoids or removes policies and practices that tend to reinforce the existence of such hierarchies.* Many such policies and practices are manifested in aspects of the physical work environment. For example, because men were predominant on the faculty of the University of Michigan Business School, the old part of the building had only one rest room per floor. As women were added, it was necessary to add rest rooms and change rest rooms previously designated for men to women's rooms or unisex rooms in order to give women equal access to these facilities. In many manufacturing plants, there are still differences of access to rest rooms for men and women, thus creating a feeling of being "second class" among women who have no facilities designated for them in their work area.

A second example comes from a manufacturing company in which the formula for computing retirement benefits produces a much larger income for people retiring from salaried jobs compared to people retiring from hourly jobs, even when they have the same seniority and average recent-year earnings. Where this exists, it is sometimes the result of union contract negotiations and thus is *not* necessarily a case of management devaluing hourly workers. Nevertheless, the mere existence of such a difference sends a message that salaried employees are more important or valuable than hourly members and reinforces a "ranking" of these classes of people.

Other examples, some of which go beyond aspects of the physical work environment, are not hard to find. Does your company have any of the following?

- Executive dining facilities or washrooms
- Reserved parking areas based on type of job
- Executive-only elevators or restricted-access office floors
- Differential vacation schedules based on type of job (for example, for people in different types of jobs with the same seniority)
- A formal specification of office furnishings based on job level or title
- Unwarranted differentiation in access to information based on job category
- Job-type restrictions on access to some forms of incentive compensation

If one or more of these exist in your company, you should ask yourself whether or not preserving these policies has benefits that outweigh the costs associated with reinforcing status hierarchies. Although it may be argued that, in rare instances, such policies are in the best interests of the total organization, in general they are unwise carryovers from a traditional organization culture that was keenly class conscious. These kinds of policies tend to build walls between people and to send unintended but enormously harmful messages about the comparative value of different kinds of people in the workplace.

In creating a culture that values diversity, these kinds of class distinctions have to be identified and cut out like a cancer.

■ Recruiting Practices

When discussing necessary changes to foster diversity, most companies have traditionally focused on how to more successfully target qualified people from underrepresented identity groups. Rather than give my spin on this well-trodden ground, I want to address recruiting processes in a different way, namely, by discussing how to shape recruiting processes for *all* new entrants to align better with managing diversity. Three areas need attention: (1) reflecting diversity competency in selection tools, (2) managing the composition of recruiting teams, and (3) conducting new-hire orientation.

Reflecting Diversity Competency in Selection Tools

If you have already been involved with organization change work related to diversity, you have probably encountered strong resistance from certain members of the workforce whose personal attitudes, beliefs, and personality traits lead them to oppose efforts to make the workplace more inclusionary of people who are different from the traditional social-cultural mix. This leads to the question: What are you doing to minimize the chances that such people continue to be hired into your organization or to be given more influence through promotions to higher levels of authority? If your answer is, "Not much, if anything," you are neglecting an important area for changes to solidify your commitment to diversity. Although I recognize that there are limitations to what can be done here, I offer the following ideas as a good start.

First, develop interview questions that ask for information about diversity competency. Here is a sample question that is now being used in certain business units of Alcoa: "Tell us about a time when you worked with someone from a different cultural background than you (for example, different gender, national origin, or race). What was the experience like for you?" Individuals who have nothing to report, who reflect a high level of discomfort with the question, or who indicate that they have had problems in the past working with people who are different would get a low score here. By contrast, people who can readily bring to mind examples and talk about them in ways that suggest they have learned something from the experiences about how to work well with people who are different should get a high score. Other people may be scored in the middle of these extremes.

This is just one example of questions that can produce useful information on previous experience with diversity issues, at least for applicants to certain kinds of jobs. A second example is to ask candidates whether they have had any previous training or educational experiences on the subject of diversity. Many high schools, colleges, and universities are offering diversity-related courses or devoting class segments to education on diversity. In addition, employers have done a great deal of training, especially since the early 1990s. Let's say you are looking at recent college graduates from top business schools, and two people stand out on the non-diversity-related criteria for your job vacancy. You then find out through your interview process that one of the two people has taken two courses in college that dealt directly with diversity. Doesn't this make that person "better qualified," given your desire to make your organization more welcoming of diversity? I think so.

A second approach for working attention to diversity into the recruiting process for all new hires is to include some diversity-related material in the selection activities that candidates are asked to complete. For example, many organizations use assessment centers to help screen candidates for jobs. By reviewing the analysis of a case dealing with diversity issues, you can learn a lot about how candidates think about the topic and perhaps something about their current skill level to resolve a diversity-related problem at work. A ready supply of such cases can be obtained from course materials used in college courses on organizational behavior and human resource management, or you can develop your own cases. Experts on diversity should be used to help you calibrate candidates' responses in terms of savvy for dealing with diversity issues.

Composition of Recruiting Teams

Some years ago, when I was working with a research and development organization, the company was concerned that its success in hiring engineers was much superior to its success in hiring persons from other disciplines. One discovery in an investigation of their recruiting process was that the team of people who did the campus recruiting and interviewed the new hires was composed almost entirely of people with engineering backgrounds. In addition, it was discovered that certain universities were disproportionately represented among persons invited for interviews and ultimately hired and that these universities were also disproportionately represented among the company's top managers. We then took steps to change the composition of the recruiting teams to broaden the types of disciplines and universities represented. This, among other changes, began to produce better results in attracting a more diverse set of new hires.

This example is a practical illustration of a phenomenon that social science scholars have labeled similarity-attraction bias or simply "similar-to-me."[2] Obviously, there are limits on the types of diversity that can be represented at high levels on a given recruiting team. However, a good mix on dimensions like gender, race, national origin, age, and work specialization among the cadre of people from which individual teams are selected is a good start.

New-Hire Orientation

There are few places where you have a greater opportunity to form a lasting impression about your commitment to making diversity an entrenched value of your organization's work culture than during the new-hire orientation process. You have a captive audience that is on ready alert to pick up signals that identify the priorities of your company. How well are you capitalizing on this opportunity?

To help you answer this question, consider for a moment company A and company B. In company A, new hires for hourly jobs get a five-minute lecture on EEO laws and a handout covering the company's sexual harassment policy. In company B, new hires get both of these things, but they also get a personal presentation by a member of the HR staff, partnered with a member of the local union leadership, who talk at length about the organization's commitment to diversity and about some of the interventions that have taken place to help make the environment diversity friendly. They then respond to questions from the new hires about everything they have heard. Which organization do you think has developed the more diversity-conscious employees?

Actually, company A and company B are the same organization, but the description of A is what the company was doing before I worked with them on organizational changes to leverage diversity; the description of company B applies to the company now. Diversity consciousness among employees is at a much higher level now than before, and the change in the orientation process is clearly a part of what made that happen. In fact, this is one of the organizations featured in Chapter Two, where I presented climate measurement data showing measured progress on changing the climate for diversity.

Many organizations are assisting new hires with their socialization into the culture of the organization by assigning them "buddies" or mentors. This can be a high-impact practice because research indicates that mentoring is very helpful to career success.[3] If you are using mentors as a part of your new-hire orientation, it is important to give attention to the implications of diversity for the mentoring process. For example, some of the research shows how critical it is for members of social-cultural minority groups to have members of the cultural majority group among their mentors. However, research also indicates that mentors serve different functions, and therefore access to a mentor who shares one's major social-cultural identities can also be helpful.[4] This research suggests that you are wise to consider the cultural identity profile of the mentor-protégé relationship among the criteria for specifying matches that will offer the best results for the new hires.

■ Performance Appraisal Practices

For most organizations seeking to improve their management of diversity, there are critical issues to be addressed in the policies and administration of formal job performance evaluations. Two of the most essential are (1) the possibility that identity factors like national origin, race, or age are affecting ratings and (2) the need to develop a meaningful way to include diversity competency as a rated item in the formal performance evaluation process. I will discuss each of these briefly.

Identity Effects on Ratings

Let me begin this section with the following question: Have you ever seen data for your organization on the average job performance ratings of employees broken down by gender, race, age, and national origin? If not, when you do see the data you might be surprised by what they show. I pose the question because extensive experience with measuring this aspect of performance evaluation in companies indicates that there is at least a fifty-fifty chance that you will find a significant difference in ratings based on one or more of these social identities. If such differences do exist, what does this mean? Answering this question is fairly complex and may ultimately require making some assumptions, but here is a sequence of steps that was used by a research and development unit of a firm in the telecommunications industry that is highly regarded for its work on diversity.

The first important step is to investigate a variety of possible causes for the finding that lend themselves to systematic data analysis. For example, if you are investigating a finding that Asians have less favorable ratings than Anglos, you might examine the educational levels, years of experience, and relevant post-hire training completed to see whether there are differences between the groups on any of these factors. If there are, then you might conclude that these differences are at least partly responsible for the differences in rated performance. Incidentally, don't be surprised if this step produces evidence that Asians actually have more rather than less education, seniority, or post-hire training than their peers at the same job level. I have found that this is fairly common. A bias that often operates in organizations is to apply higher-than-normal standards for education or experience when assessing members of cultural minority groups for hiring or promotion.

If this first step produces no basis for the difference in ratings, then attention must turn to the process of creating the ratings. Here the investigation gets much dicier. At this juncture there are two main possibilities: (1) factors in the work climate make it more difficult for Asians than for Anglos to achieve their full potential for performance, and (2) raters are scoring Asians lower for the same displayed performance level. Keeping in mind that barriers like stereotyping, prejudice, and ethnocentrism can actually reduce performance, we have to investigate the *possibility* that Asians, as a group, are indeed performing at a lower level than Anglos, despite having equal qualifications. This is essentially explanation 1. Alternatively, these same human tendencies can be manifested in the form of biased performance ratings, especially if the vast majority of raters are not Asian. To make things even more complicated, cultural differences between Anglos and many Asian groups can play a part in rating fairness. For example, if self-evaluations are a part of the rating process, persons with roots in cultures that stress modesty, such as the Korean, Chinese, and Japanese cultures, may not represent their accomplishments as strongly as Anglos and thereby hurt themselves in the rating process. This set of issues is embedded in explanation 2.

This is as far as we got with my example telecommunications firm. Because they could find no differences in qualifications that would account for differences in performance, they concluded that some form of bias was entering the rating process. One additional step that can be taken is to look at data on the climate for diversity, especially diversity of national origin and race. If the measures indicate that the climate is strongly supportive of these forms of diversity, in ways other than race-correlated performance ratings, there is a greater chance that explanation 2 applies.

Although sorting out explanation 1 from explanation 2 is tricky business, the need to make this difficult distinction is lessened by the fact that certain action steps can address both causes. The company can, for example, institute a strong series of communications and educational interventions designed to heighten awareness and change behaviors related to the possible effects of cultural identity group differences on both the ability to perform at one's best and the rating process itself.

Diversity as a Criterion in Performance Ratings

Most organizations use some type of formal appraisal of job performance for all personnel in salaried jobs and sometimes also for people in hourly jobs. If your organization is using them, you may be struggling with finding an effective way to bring diversity *competency* into this process. Even if your organization is not using formal job performance ratings, it is still important to provide feedback to individual employees on how well they are supporting the diversity-related goals of your firm. My experience is that including diversity competency in job performance appraisal in a way that has high meaning and impact is easier said than done. Nevertheless, it is possible to make significant improvement on past practice by following a few straightforward steps.

First, study the architecture of the performance appraisal process to determine how best to integrate diversity content. To illustrate this point, Figure 6.1 shows the basic structure of the performance management process currently used by Alcoa.

The performance management process includes the following:

- *Planning* is a joint effort between an employee and his or her manager to (1) define individual roles based on business objectives, (2) determine annual individual objectives, and (3) identify the critical success factors and business-technical knowledge required to excel in the identified role.
- *Assessment* is a determination of what has been accomplished during the previous time period, how it has been accomplished, and what further development would enhance performance. An outcome of this is a job performance rating. The three types of factors assessed are those indicated in the planning segment: objectives, knowledge, and success factors.

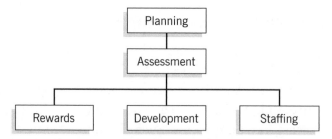

Figure 6.1. **Structure of the Performance Management Plan of Alcoa (circa 2000)**

The assessment process includes collecting data from peers, direct reports, customers, and supervisors in addition to the person him- or herself through a 360-degree feedback mechanism. Information from comparison of the assessment with the planned achievements will determine the other three elements of the process (that is, the *rewards* one will receive, what further *development* is needed, and what *staffing decisions* may need to occur).

Until recently, diversity competency was not directly represented in this process. As a consequence the behaviors and accomplishments of individuals in relation to the diversity objectives of the business were not being planned, assessed, or used for specification of performance management outcomes in any systematic way. Since then, some business units of the company have adopted the outline shown in Table 6.2 to change the performance management process to incorporate attention to diversity competency.

In the "success factor" segment of Alcoa's performance management process there is a lot of focus on specific behaviors; a focus on behaviors is recommended by performance management experts. Accordingly, I suggest that you give thought to what specific behaviors you want to encourage from your employees in order to foster a climate that is supportive of diversity. Table 6.3 offers a sample of behaviors that were specified for use in the Alcoa business units that have been the focus of my case illustration. Most of these behaviors have application in organizations of all types. By including some specific behaviors that distinguish good from poor performance in the performance management process, managers using the process gain a valuable tool to help establish diversity competence in the work groups that they supervise, and employees get much needed guidelines for self-development efforts.

Table 6.2. **Changes to Performance Management to Incorporate Diversity**

1. There is an expectation that diversity competency will be addressed whenever possible in all three major components of the planning process: objectives, business knowledge, and success factors.

   Examples for Objectives: A manager might set a goal to (1) increase the representation of women in her area of responsibility by "X" percent or (2) improve the retention rate for women by a specified amount, or (3) establish mentoring relationships with two people who are culturally different from himself or herself.

   Examples for the Building Knowledge component: Specify the type of knowledge needed: (1) understand ways in which gender affects communication styles and effectiveness, (2) know the legal requirements of a nonhostile work environment, (3) understand the potential performance benefits of a diverse workforce, (4) learn techniques for defusing a conflict at work that is related to race or ethnic differences.

   The Success Factor component is addressed in item 4.

2. The set of respondents selected to provide rounded feedback should, whenever possible, be diverse as to gender, race, national origin, age, work specialization, and other diversity factors.

3. Diversity competency should be represented in individual development plans.

4. A success factor is added for "valuing diversity," and attention to diversity will be given in assessing other success factors such as communicating, developing others, and resolving conflicts.

■ **Career Development Practices**

Aligning career development practices with the goal of diversity competency requires giving attention to a variety of issues. Some of the most important are job posting, annual development planning, succession planning, and (for multinational firms) the globalization of career paths. I will offer some tips for effectiveness in each of these areas.

Table 6.3. Behaviors for the Assessment of the "Values Diversity" Success Factor

1. Intervenes to stop others from using slurs, telling offensive jokes, or displaying other inappropriate behaviors

2. Openly expresses support for diversity-related goals of the company

3. Invites feedback from colleagues on behavior that is related to diversity competency

4. Accepts or volunteers for diversity-related work assignments (for example, to join a diversity task force, be a diversity trainer, or serve on civil rights complaints committees)

5. Interacts effectively with people who are culturally different from himself or herself

6. Seeks out persons who are culturally different for informal contact (for example, for lunches or for break-time or after-work activities)

7. Brings diversity-related problems or opportunities to the attention of higher levels of management

8. Mentors people who are culturally different from himself or herself

9. Promotes stronger relationships between union and salaried employees

10. Participates enthusiastically in diversity-related education activities (for example, attends nonmandatory training and displays a high level of participation during training)

Job Posting

Unless your company is very small, a well-implemented job-posting plan will help you achieve your diversity goals. *Job posting* means publicizing job openings to all current employees for a specified period of time and guaranteeing that anyone who responds will get due consideration for selection.

Job posting is recommended by the most knowledgeable people as a staple of world-class career development systems and thus is a good thing for all employees, but the existence of diversity makes its use much more valuable. This is because it is one of the most effective ways to reduce the actual and imaginary advantages of cultural majority group members for being selected to fill vacancies with internal candidates. To illustrate the point, some years ago I was interviewing a high-level manager of an oil company as part of a culture assessment project. As part of my study of the selection processes in the company, I asked the manager how he happened to come into the position that he currently held. He responded that a friend in the business unit, with whom he had worked before, had specifically asked for him to fill the job and had called his former supervisor to see if he could be released to take it. This is not an infrequent scenario and, in and of itself, there is nothing sinister about it. However, as we know from published research, this kind of informal, network-based selection puts members of cultural minority groups at a distinct disadvantage because they are simply less likely to have a friend in high places who will ask for them by name.[5]

Well-executed job posting will help your diversity effort in at least three ways. First, it makes opportunities more visible so that qualified members of all identity groups can apply for them. In this regard, I frequently hear from minority culture members that they see jobs being filled by others that they did not even know were vacant. Second, posting jobs requires a competitive screening process that must be defended for fairness and therefore increases the chances of due diligence of consideration of all qualified applicants. This tends to level the playing field in terms of the kind of selection that occurred with the manager in my oil firm example. Finally, a properly executed job-posting plan requires specific feedback to applicants on why someone else was selected in preference to them. This reduces the probability that your employees will attribute nonselection to some identity factor like gender, disability, or national origin.

Annual Development Planning

Another staple of world-class career development processes is the use of annual individual development plans. These plans specify the skills and competencies that need to be strengthened during the coming year, along with an action plan for acquiring them. When properly done, the specification of development needs is not limited to the current job but includes a target job that matches with the individual's short-term career goals.

An obvious use of this tool is to help increase the pool of qualified members of underrepresented identity groups for expected future job vacancies. If you are not already doing individual development plans annually, I suggest that you do so. It will enhance your overall effort to invest in people as the most important element of your organization, and it will give you a critical tool for leveraging diversity. If you are already using annual development plans effectively in your organization to increase the pipeline of qualified people from underrepresented groups, I pose to you a different challenge. Gather a random sample of a few dozen copies of the most recently completed development plans for people in your company and look for evidence of diversity competency as a development need or part of the action-planning segment. My experience suggests that you will probably find little or no evidence that diversity competency is an important performance requirement in your company. If this is what you find, it is an important wake-up call for your organization.

I have already given some ideas on assessing diversity competency. The follow-up issue here is what kind of action steps can be suggested to someone who really wants to work on diversity competency. To help with this, Table 6.4 gives a list of possibilities that I have developed in work with organizations on this issue. Some of the ideas are not relevant for all job categories, but the list should give you a good start toward a strong menu of possibilities.

Table 6.4. **Sample Items for Development Plans**

1. Attend diversity training.

2. Perform community work with organizations primarily serving people who are culturally different.

3. Participate in off-site dialogue meetings on diversity.

4. Participate in on-site dialogue meetings on diversity.

5. Read "X" number of books or articles on diversity.

6. Apply for an overseas assignment.

7. Travel to countries with different cultures.

8. Enroll in college or executive education courses on diversity.

9. Attend a national or local conference on workplace diversity.

10. Organize a diversity conference for your organization.

11. Author or coauthor an article or case study on a diversity-related topic (for example, for a company newsletter article).

12. Learn a new language.

13. Pursue a job assignment in a work unit with a substantially different demographic profile or a job involving managing diversity duties.

Succession Planning

Succession planning involves identifying individuals in an organization who are potential replacements for people occupying key jobs and ensuring that they get the development they need to fill these jobs. The outcome of succession planning is to create depth in the organization of highly qualified people at least for a specified set of critical jobs. Although traditionally the emphasis of succession planning was on a limited number of higher-level jobs, the smarter firms are doing succession planning for a broader set of jobs, starting at middle management or even lower. To bring a priority on cultural diversity into this process two steps are essential.

First, it is necessary to monitor the profile of succession planning candidate pools for diversity on key dimensions like gender, race, national origin, and work specialization. The last dimension is necessary to avoid scenarios such as limiting access to top jobs to people with certain professional specialties. Depending on the company, engineering, marketing, and finance are ones that I commonly see. Organizations that are world class on managing diversity routinely require gender, race, and (where appropriate) national origin diversity in succession planning pools. But doing so means that priority must be placed on diversity for experienced new hires, and especially in development processes for current employees.

The second requirement for bringing attention to diversity into succession planning processes is to ensure that possible successors for key jobs are diversity-competent. Unfortunately, only a small percentage of companies take this seriously. This effort must start at the very top of the organization. CEOs and other leaders who are committed to changing the culture of their organizations to be better at welcoming and using diversity must make sure that the people most likely to replace them are strong on managing diversity. I don't think this is as difficult as some leaders that I've talked to make it out to be. If you are knowledgeable about the topic of diversity, you can learn a lot about the suitability of potential replacements by listening to how they talk about diversity issues and change efforts and by watching their level of effort on diversity initiatives in the areas of the organization that they are currently managing. You can also ask for input from a diverse set of colleagues who can not only give their own views about potential candidates but gather intelligence from others as well. Add to this any formal data that are available as a result of including diversity competence in performance appraisal forms, and a very formidable set of information can be created.

Global Career Path Issues

As noted in Chapter One, the globalization of business is a trend that makes diversity competency crucial for many organizations. Although the term *multinational* conjures up images of huge companies like Alcoa, many small companies derive a large proportion of their revenues from other countries of the world.

If you are working for a firm that has multinational product services or labor markets, several critical issues lie at the intersection of diversity and career development; perhaps the most basic is whether your firm is doing enough to provide multinational career paths for high-potential employees. This is a critical step toward preparing such people to perform successfully in a business that is increasingly diverse on the dimension of national origin.

Let me quickly acknowledge here that it often makes sense from a cost standpoint to leave the management of off-shore operations to locals. There are also certain operational benefits that may be well served by this strategy. For example, a more refined knowledge of the local culture may avoid some potential pitfalls, and it is important for locals to see that the top jobs in the company are open to people born in their country. For all of these reasons the "leave it to the locals" strategy is popular today in multinational companies. However, from a career development standpoint, there is a serious downside to taking this strategy too far. Without the cross-fertilization of moving people among the different countries represented in the firm, it is difficult to provide the breadth of experience that the ideal candidate for high-level jobs should have. Therefore, I advocate a balanced approach in which the desire to have the top jobs open to locals and the desire for multinational career paths are both given high priority.

It is important to point out that the benefits of multinational career paths should go beyond the personal development of the individuals who take these assignments. Also crucial is that the knowledge they gain should be systematically passed on to others to aid their development. By doing this, the increase of diversity competency that comes from these assignments can be pushed deeper into the organization.[6]

A related issue is the question of who has access to global career paths. To the extent that experience working in multiple countries is important for promotion to top jobs in your organization, you must take steps to ensure that people of all social-cultural identity groups have the opportunity for these jobs. In my experience, this equal opportunity for expatriate assignments does not always happen. One example that has received some exposure in published material is the tendency in many firms to favor men over women for such assignments. A less well-known but still important example is the tendency for firms to give greater access to multinational career paths to people who are natives of the host country. For example, many firms based in the United States do a better job of rounding out the experience of their U.S.-born high-potential managers than they do with managers born in other countries.

A variation on this was illustrated in a recent conversation I had with a manager from a Jamaican-based business unit of a large, U.S.-based multinational company. In our discussion about what the company was doing to help prepare people to take assignments in another country, this manager pointed out that the limited training that was being done was directed almost exclusively toward people going *from* the United States to other nations. People like himself who were born outside the United States got little or no help in understanding U.S. culture when they were assigned to jobs in the United States. This is a subtle but undeniable form of unequal opportunity that too often occurs.

CHAPTER SUMMARY

I am often asked by managers of organizations frustrated with their inability to achieve lasting change on their diversity goals: "Why haven't we been able to see better results?" If you are asking this question, the work described in this chapter on taking a systems approach is a big part of the answer. Three areas that require attention are time policies, space policies, and people process policies. Within each area a myriad of specific issues must be assessed through the "lens of diversity" to see how they might be changed to better reflect the demands of a diverse workforce. Some examples and tools have been given here to help you start this work. By recognizing the interdependence among elements of the organization and working conscientiously to align them all more tightly with the implications of increasing diversity of people, you will begin to see powerful change take hold in your organization.

Questions for Further Learning and Development

1. Using the list of climate factors in Table 6.1, identify and discuss ways in which they are affected by or related to workforce diversity. This is essentially a task of extending the type of analysis given throughout the chapter to (1) address the nine factors not included among the sample items discussed in the chapter and (2) add additional insights or customize the analysis that I have given, for the first five factors that are discussed.
2. Many of the changes to the "time factors" of Table 6.1 that would be called for to promote workforce diversity (for example, eliminating forced overtime and increasing part-time work) are somewhat at odds with the trends in many organizations toward longer hours. How can the need to be more flexible on time committed to paid employment be balanced with the need to "do more faster and with fewer people" that defines the culture of many of today's organizations?
3. Use the sample behaviors in Table 6.3 to do a mini-assessment of your own diversity competency. What are your areas of strength and weakness? Create a plan for building on strengths and eliminating weaknesses.
4. Using a relevant combination of gender, race, and national origin, do an "identity profile" of your work colleagues who are *ready now* to replace you in your current job. If this group is culturally homogeneous, what needs to be done to change that?
5. How much work has already been done in your organization to align people systems with the goals of welcoming and leveraging diversity? Which of the process-practice areas of Table 6.1 should be the focus of attention in the next twelve months?

Follow Up for Sustainable Results

A s I do work in companies on organizational change, I frequently conduct interviews with employees to learn about the current work environment and to ask for their help to create the change that is needed to take the organization to a higher level of effectiveness. Some themes recur in these discussions with amazing frequency. One of the most frequent and most deadly is that people see the change effort on diversity as just another "flavor of the month." They say that leaders are always launching activity toward some espoused vision but that they fail to maintain any consistency of attention to the change objectives. They say that leaders talk a good game but have yet to deliver results. As a consequence of these beliefs there is an unmistakable attitude of "we've heard it all before and don't believe any of it." If this sounds familiar to you, and especially if your honest assessment is that there is good reason for this kind of skepticism, you are working in an organization with a follow-up problem.

Here's a quick test to further check out your company on this point. Think of the last major change effort that occurred in your organization. Perhaps it was devoted to establishing total quality or self-managed work teams or work process reengineering. Locate the list of action steps that were approved for implementation. You know you are in deep trouble if you can't recall or locate such a list. Assuming that you find one, check off the steps that have actually been *fully* implemented and then compute a rate of implementation by dividing completed items by the total number on the list. Chances are you will come up with a figure of less than 50 percent.

In this chapter, I offer some suggestions for avoiding the pitfalls of poor follow-up and for establishing effective follow-up and accountability when doing work on diversity. My suggestions call for four specific actions: (1) use a plan review, (2) keep score, (3) provide incentives for positive behavior, and (4) manage knowledge retention and transfer.

■ The Plan Review Process

The ubiquitous problem of lack of follow-up on change initiatives occurs in part because many top leaders deal with diversity strategy only by communicating a set of values and expectations such as "We will show respect to all people," "We will ensure equal opportunity," "We will not tolerate harassment," "We will value the richness of diversity," and so on. They then leave the implementation of these goals to others, assuming that people will follow through. They fail to understand that making these goals a part of the culture will require a deployment process and that *it is up to them to make sure the process is being used.*

More effective leadership will require top leaders to proactively establish real accountability for results on diversity with their direct reports. The result will be that accountability will cascade down through the organization, leading to the kind of comprehensive follow-up effort that is needed to make change happen.

A major tool that top leaders can use to create this cascading effect is the planning review process. Most organizations have some such process already in place for the discussion of financial goals and plans such as sales targets, new product development, budgets, and the like. A common scenario is that a round of meetings is held at various organizational levels each quarter. Recognizing the folly of disconnecting planning for financial goals from other key elements of the business strategy, many organizations are also requiring a discussion of plans for people during these business plan review meetings. What is missing for many firms is a *substantive* review in these meetings of plans related to diversity goals.

Please note the emphasis on the word *substantive.* Simply reviewing the latest data on the gender, race, and nationality profile of people in jobs above a certain job grade is woefully insufficient. Although it is important for top leaders to review such data on a regular basis, limiting the review of diversity goals in this way is problematic for several reasons. First, although knowing current numbers on demographic profiles is useful and necessary, it is even more important to know what is being done to improve them. Second, as emphasized throughout this book, the change effort for creating an environment for diversity requires action on a broader scope. Third, it is necessary to evaluate the extent to which the organization is following a *process* that brings some degree of consistency to the effort and that is likely to lead to success.

If you are a senior leader who conducts quarterly business plan reviews or if you are coaching someone who will review business plans dealing with diversity goals, Table 7.1 gives a sample of questions that you might ask. The table is based on the assumption that you are using the five-step change model depicted in this book.

Asking questions like those listed can tell you in a hurry who is really working the change process and who is just bluffing. I am reminded here of a conversation I had recently with the president of one of Alcoa's business units. He told me he had just had his quarterly review meeting with then-CEO Paul O'Neill and that he was struck by the fact that even though his unit was among the best in the world on safety performance, he still got a full half-hour of heavy questioning from Paul about what he was doing on safety. This story left me with several impressions, but two major ones are (1) you have to know an area well in order to ask the tough questions and really do the job on follow-up and accountability for change, and (2) we must establish a norm of continuous improvement for critical goals lest we fall into complacency when things are going well. Regarding the first point, it is terribly important that leaders invest the time to learn enough about diversity to ask detailed questions

Table 7.1. Sample Questions for Plan Review Meetings

1. What is your plan for education on diversity?
2. Who in your organization is developing some expertise on this subject?
3. What measures of success are you using?
4. Where are you in the measurement process, and if far enough along, what results are you getting?
5. What are you doing to maintain a high level of communication on the diversity effort?
6. Give an example of what you are doing on HR policy and practice alignment this year. What is the status of your work in this area?
7. What can we do at the enterprise level to support your work better?

during planning reviews and to avoid being victimized by smoke-and-mirror artists. It is equally important for them to take some responsibility for investigating *how* people are pursuing change, for example, by asking specifically about the deployment of the change *process* and not just about what *results* are being achieved. This is especially important in the early stages when there may not be much on results achieved to talk about. During the early stages, the focus of attention is on the likelihood of achieving results, and this is where knowing that people are using the process becomes essential.

Before leaving this topic, I want to say another word about the issue of continuous improvement. Years ago in manufacturing firms, one would commonly hear quality goals stated in terms of percent reject rates of .5 to 5 or higher. Delivery performance was likewise targeted at some specified percent, usually well below 100. Today in world-class manufacturing organizations one hears these goals stated as the right product, on time, every time. Quality goals are understood to be zero defects. I think it makes sense to apply the same philosophy to managing diversity. How acceptable is it to have a sexual harassment rate of 10 percent or 5 percent, or to have, say, 80 percent of the workforce feel respected and valued? At what level of favorable climate for diversity does the work end? I believe we have to take the position that harassment of even a few people is not acceptable and that the experience of being respected at work must apply to everyone. Norms of continuous improvement dictate that the work on diversity is never done. We just keep refining it and journeying to ever-higher levels of achievement.

■ Keeping Score

An old axiom in organizational work is that "you get what you measure." I have found that this statement applies very well to managing diversity work. Companies like Xerox, DuPont, and

Motorola have made exceptional progress on breaking the glass ceiling for women and racial-minority men, in part because of their vigorous efforts to measure the workforce profiles against meticulously maintained data on the qualified labor pool for frequently filled jobs. The success of these and similar companies highlights both the strengths and the perils of keeping score by means of EEO data. An approach emphasizing such clearly defined measurements can help keep managers focused on the diversity of candidate pools and on decision making for hiring and promotions. But it is also true that when we limit our score keeping to demographic profile data, there is often little or no attention to other aspects of the climate for diversity. The flip side of "You get what you measure" is "You don't get what you don't measure."

Keeping score is important for facilitating more precise goal setting and for strengthening performance management efforts, but it is also important for another, less often recognized, reason. In much of the world, and certainly in the highly industrialized nations of the Western Hemisphere, there is a human need to measure the results of what one is accomplishing against some known yardstick of goodness. David McClelland's classic research on the achievement motive provides some of the best-known evidence in support of this statement.[1] People will work harder on the goals of your diversity change effort if they have some tangible targets to shoot for and if they can see how they are doing, partly because they just feel better when there is tangible evidence of achievement. The psychological and emotional value of keeping score, even if early results are not encouraging, should not be underestimated.

In Chapter Four I offered ideas on types of measures for diversity work and discussed pitfalls to avoid and suggestions for success in creating formal measurement plans. There I addressed measurement in the traditional (and I think essential) sense of keeping score "by the numbers." I also emphasized the point that the score card should not be one-dimensional. A mixture of metrics such as demographic profile data, percent change on survey data, employee turnover rates, and percent of plans implemented on time should be used to set goals, determine performance, and provide a basis for the distribution of performance incentives related to managing diversity. More will be said shortly about using incentives. First, however, I want to add to the material of Chapter Four by briefly discussing a different kind of measurement that I call "keeping score by walking around."

Keeping Score by Walking Around

It is often said that a picture is worth a thousand words. In the domain of leading and managing organizations we should probably add to this, "as long as there are a thousand words and numbers somewhere to back up the picture." Nevertheless, I believe it is true that a lot of us measure how things are going by visual images. For example, the dean of the University of Michigan Business School, Joe White, tells the story of a former CEO of Cummings Engine, who, after walking into a room full of U.S.-born white, male engineers, asked his VP of human resources, "What's wrong with this picture?" The VP replied that it was too homogeneous on some visible dimensions of human diversity. The story goes that the CEO then explained that it was also evidence of a quality problem because the best people in the world to do the jobs that were represented were not all white, male engineers. His point was well taken, but the point I'd like to make with this story is that by walking into a room where people of certain job types are gathered, one can gauge, without actually counting heads, one important aspect of how the organization is doing on diversity goals.

Now consider a different example of keeping score by walking around. After several years of work on valuing diversity had been completed at Digital Equipment, a colleague of mine made a visit there to learn about what they were doing. She related to me how impressed she was with their core group effort and other things, but she was also struck by how the work climate, in her words, "felt very different" from the climate of her own organization. When I pressed her on what she meant, she gave the example of seeing clusters of employees of different types of jobs—management and hourly, different departments, different levels of authority, and so on—gathering in conversation in hallways, at lunch tables, and in vending areas.

For still another example of keeping score by walking around, consider the possibility of making the numbers that are tracked on diversity goals more visible. To illustrate, I am reminded of a visit to a plant of Northern Telecom in Tennessee about ten years ago. The plant was investing heavily in the implementation of a total quality process, and this was obvious from all the signs and graphs posted showing the latest quality results for various units of the plants. Just by walking and looking around I got a good idea of how the plant was doing on quality. The same can be done for diversity.

A final example of keeping score by walking around is to use the informal feedback from employees that you get as you walk around your place of work as a way to gauge whether or not the climate is improving. As I have already discussed, the use of survey data has distinct advantages for formal measurement of progress, but there are definite limitations on how frequently you want to use surveys (I suggest no more than once per year). In the interim you can get useful informal measures by going out and talking to people about what they see and what they think regarding the climate for diversity. This way of keeping score has residual advantages such as adding another mechanism for two-way, verbal communication, which, in my experience, is the most valued form of communication for most employees.

■ Providing Incentives for New Behaviors

Decades of research on human motivation,[2] as well as my personal experiences working with companies, suggests that the impact of keeping score on behavior is greatly intensified when scores generate consequences that are important to people. Three types of consequences that should be considered here are monetary rewards, personal or work-group recognition, and opportunities for advancement.

Monetary Rewards

Like many organizations, Alcoa has an incentive compensation plan that provides a level of monetary compensation beyond the base salary, with the amount contingent on job performance for a given year. For higher-level executives, such as the heads of business units, it is not unusual for the potential amount of money at stake for such contingency rewards to be hundreds of thousands of dollars. Even middle managers commonly have tens of thousands of dollars riding on performance on key strategic goals. If this kind of incentive compensation is available in your organization, it should be leveraged as a motivational tool to get the work on managing diversity done at a high level of quality and at a reasonable pace. One example of this was given in Chapter Three, where I mentioned the Alcoa executive who made a percentage of the compensation for his direct reports (business unit heads) dependent on the demonstration of a successful launch of the change process on diversity for their respective business units. A successful launch was defined in specific terms, which included a requirement for completion of a high-quality culture assessment. The units involved all followed through with a request for assistance from my consulting group for help with climate assessment work (discussed in Chapter Four), and they were off to a good start on working the process model.

I want to emphasize the point that providing incentives for positive behavior in this way is not effective simply because people are motivated by the opportunity to earn more money. Many of the business unit heads in my Alcoa example already earn more than enough money to satisfy their needs in base salary alone. The key here is that, by linking a portion of the incentive compensation to diversity goals, the leader is sending a message that the accomplishment of these goals is essential to success as an organization. It establishes the priority of the goals relating to diversity, and it establishes the proper kind of alignment between goals and the rewards of achievement. This creates a *coherence of leadership behavior* that generates a lot of focus among managers on the specified priorities for that planning period. Alternatively, to *say* that the accomplishment of diversity goals is essential while leaving these goals out of the incentive compensation formulas sends a mixed message and substantially weakens the level of focus on the goals involved. Unfortunately, the latter scenario is what I find most frequently, despite the fact that leading firms on diversity change—Corning, Allstate, Motorola, and others—have been using monetary incentives in the way prescribed here for years. I find that this point about monetary incentives for performance on diversity goals being effective is lost on many executives who ask me, "Why do we need to pay people to do what is right?" or "Why should there be special incentives for people just doing their jobs?" In response to such questions, I like to point out that the same objections apply to performance on other organizational goals, including direct financial goals.

Of course, this line of discussion invariably brings us to the question of how one measures performance on managing diversity. Some help on this was given in Chapter Four. To be sure, much work remains to be done to refine the available metrics for use in diversity change work. Equally valid is the argument that measurements on the organization's capability to leverage diversity are often less tangible than financial performance measures like sales and costs. Nevertheless, we should not let these limitations become excuses for not using incentives for positive behaviors to manage diversity.

So far in this section I have been discussing how to provide monetary incentives through incentive compensation, but in many organizations incentive compensation is limited to employees in certain kinds of salaried jobs. A common scenario, for example, is to limit participation in incentive compensation to middle- and higher-level managers. It is especially challenging to find adequate ways to use monetary rewards for performance on managing diversity goals for people in lower-level jobs such as hourly employees or clerical staff. Fortunately, other forms of incentives may be used that do not have the same limitations as incentive compensation. I will discuss these under the general heading of personal and group recognition.

Personal and Group Recognition

When was the last time you or someone else in your organization received some form of public recognition for exemplary performance related to the goals of managing diversity? If you're like most people, you can't remember ever seeing this, and this is a major, lost opportunity. Here are a few ideas for recognizing behaviors that represent excellence in managing diversity:

- Annual awards for leadership on managing diversity
- Paid days off for best ideas to further the managing diversity agenda
- Diversity champion awards

Annual leadership awards would recognize individuals in leadership roles who have demonstrated exceptional contribution toward the vision for diversity. An example would be an annual CEO award for diversity excellence. This would be awarded to one or more individuals who have been identified through a nomination process, with the selection being made by the CEO of the company upon advice by some designated group of diversity-knowledgeable people such as a diversity steering or advisory committee. The award might consist of a certificate and some high-profile publicity, including a ceremony in which the award is personally given by the CEO with his or her expressions of appreciation. This type of recognition may also include a modest monetary award, which is recommended but not mandatory.

The value of this kind of incentive goes beyond the benefits of individual recognition. The existence of such an award reinforces the message that managing diversity is a high priority for the organization. It also provides a mechanism for connecting the CEO of the firm with people at other levels of the organization with whom he or she would otherwise not come into contact.

Offering an incentive like paid days off for the best ideas relating to the organization's diversity goals also has multiple benefits. It increases motivation to work on diversity goals while stimulating other things that organizations want to increase, such as employee involvement and creativity. Although this kind of recognition can be effective with a variety of recognition elements, I have found that workers today are especially attracted to the opportunity to be recognized by having a little additional time off. Of course, like all incentives, this requires some kind of selection process. The key here is to involve people in nomination and selection who really know the diversity-related performance of the people being considered. An example is that if this recognition effort is intended to consider workers in all job categories, which is what I strongly recommend, you will need to have a cross-sectional group of very carefully selected people from various jobs to decide who gets recognized.

As criteria for selection will be needed, you might want to consider using an explicit inventory of positive diversity behaviors. For help with this point, please see the examples presented in Chapters Three and Six.

Opportunities for Advancement

Let me say at the outset that I view promotions as being first and foremost a method for filling job vacancies with the most qualified candidates available and secondarily as a means of developing people. I do *not* think promotions are best viewed as mechanisms of reward. Rewards should be given based on past performance in the current job, whereas promotions should be given only to people who have done an outstanding job in their current position *and* have shown a strong potential to do jobs at higher levels of responsibility and authority. Having said this, I think it is appropriate and necessary, in all promotion decisions, to give substantial consideration to people's ability to manage diversity well. When this is in place, enhancing one's prospects for promotion becomes another incentive for learning and displaying positive behaviors for managing diversity.

When the vision for diversity is fully realized, it should be commonplace for a candidate's reputation for dealing with diversity to be discussed at length during meetings where people are being evaluated for promotion or where their potential to do higher-level jobs is addressed. This is an extremely important accountability item, not only because of the incentive value of promotions but because people need to be screened on diversity competency in order to avoid putting people who are obstacles to the vision for diversity in positions of increased influence. Ideas for evaluating diversity competency were given in Chapter Six on management systems alignment.

A very critical matter that arises in this context is the question of whether diversity competence will be treated as a *threshold* factor or simply as a *portfolio* factor when evaluating people for promotion. To illustrate, consider an experience I had while working with a large auto manufacturer. Candidates to replace the general manager of the division included a man I'll call Jim. Jim had all the right qualifications in other areas but was spoken of by many female employees as a person who "had a problem relating to women," especially in professional roles. The question to be answered is, Should Jim's shortcoming on diversity be considered as one factor among many (the portfolio approach), in which case there is a good chance he may still be selected, or should he be eliminated from further consideration on the basis of his lack of competency on diversity issues alone (the threshold approach)? My advice is that diversity competence should be treated as a threshold factor. Of course, this opinion assumes that there is significant credible evidence of an ongoing behavior deficiency in the area of managing diversity.

I hasten to add that this threshold treatment of diversity competency in promotion decisions also means that people can be selected as well as excluded, based on reputation and performance results related to managing diversity. The factor that sets a person apart from his or her peers may well be a reputation for consistently dealing with people of different cultural backgrounds in an effective manner and otherwise demonstrating support of the company's diversity goals.

The ability for advancement opportunity to serve as an incentive for positive diversity behaviors clearly depends on how well your organization executes some of the other ideas that have been presented in this book, in particular the suggestions for including diversity competence in performance appraisal and in recruiting processes. This discussion also reminds us of how valuable it is for employees to be given help with the development of diversity competency—a topic I addressed to some degree in Chapters Five and Six.

Before leaving this section, I should point out that I have deliberately emphasized establishing accountability for good performance on diversity by reinforcing positive behavior, as opposed to reacting to negative behavior. However, the flip side of taking corrective action for negative performance is implied. Accountability is strongest when the extremes of both positive and negative behavior elicit strong consequences.

■ Managing Knowledge Retention and Transfer

In recent years, the management of knowledge has become a focus of increasing attention in organizations. Companies that have been active in this area include General Electric, British Petroleum, Ford Motor Company, and the consulting firm of Booz•Allen & Hamilton. As an indication of how serious some companies are about this effort, Booze Allen is among those that have created a high-level position with the title of chief knowledge officer (CKO). The interest in knowledge management is occurring in part because organizations have learned that being more efficient at learning and sharing information, and especially at sharing experience, can be a significant competitive advantage.[3]

What I want to do here is illustrate how the concept of knowledge management is highly relevant to work on managing diversity and offer some ideas for its application in this field. Let me begin by providing some background on the concept of knowledge management.

Basics of Knowledge Management

The term *knowledge management* is being used to label a system to promote the sharing of knowledge throughout an organization or constellation of organizations. According to leading experts, knowledge management has the following objectives:[4]

- Make the process of knowledge creation explicit.
- Involve customers in processes to increase their satisfaction with results (for example, get input from customers on new products at various stages of development).
- Add knowledge to a process in order to increase customer value.
- Share knowledge more effectively.
- Improve the execution of programs and initiatives.

For my purposes the last two items are especially relevant. I will return to them shortly.

Researchers have also identified a number of key success factors for implementing effective knowledge management systems. These factors are shown in Table 7.2.

With this background in mind, I next talk briefly about the objectives and requirements of knowledge management programs, as they relate to managing diversity. I will then offer some suggestions on how to manage knowledge of diversity-related change efforts. Much of what I have to say here is especially applicable to large organizations.

Table 7.2. Key Success Factors for Knowledge Management Systems[5]

1. Senior management support
2. A uniform yet flexible knowledge structure (includes a specific taxonomy for organizing knowledge and a standardized process for sharing it)
3. A clear objective for knowledge sharing
4. The use of clear language
5. A culture that is supportive of sharing knowledge
6. Rewards and incentives that reinforce knowledge sharing
7. Multiple channels for sharing knowledge
8. Technical and human resources to support the system (for example, properly designed computer information systems)
9. Measurement of system effectiveness and its value in terms of firm performance

Application of Knowledge Management to Managing Diversity

As I mentioned, two foundational elements of knowledge management are objectives and key factors for success. Each of these will be addressed here.

Objectives of Knowledge Management
Of the five objectives for knowledge management previously listed, I find that the last two apply particularly well to managing diversity efforts, namely, (1) sharing knowledge more effectively and (2) improving the execution of programs and initiatives. Actually, these two objectives are highly interrelated, and I view the first as leading to the second. In large organizations, the ability to rapidly transfer knowledge from one part of the organization to other parts is a critical competitive factor. For enterprisewide change efforts like managing diversity, it is important to have good knowledge transfer to avoid the problem of duplication of effort and to ensure that the best ideas are leveraged to help other units without any unnecessary loss of time.

Despite the obvious benefits of sharing knowledge about managing diversity efforts, I have often found that the experience of specific subunits of organizations (departments, divisions, business units, and so on) is *not* readily available to other units. This problem is exacerbated when there is no enterprise-level resource for coordinating work on managing diversity, but in very large multinational companies like General Electric and General Motors, even the presence of such a role has not entirely solved it. Examples of when better sharing of knowledge is needed include training programs and work on aligning HR processes. To illustrate, consider these recent examples from my work with Alcoa. The Wenatche manufacturing plant of Alcoa's Primary Metals business unit created an educational program on workplace harassment that has received very positive reviews from the workforce. However, even though dozens of the company's operations are trying to develop effective teaching activities on harassment, many of them were slow to learn about the Wenatche effort. As a second example, consider a vice president of human resources of a company recently acquired by Alcoa. He is trying to implement the HR systems alignment component of the change model presented in this book and is looking for help. Even though work has already been done with other units of the company on the HR systems of performance appraisal, career development, and recruiting, he does not know about this work and has no easy way to learn about it. Fortunately, in both of these examples, all of the organizational units involved were using the same outside consultant; this provided a mechanism for transferring knowledge. Still, there are flaws in this approach to knowledge transfer. The first is that it is not unusual for units of the same organization to use different consultants and, for competitive and other reasons, the amount of cross-fertilization among consultants working on the same strategic area is typically minuscule. This point highlights a subtle but significant disadvantage to the proliferation of consulting groups among units of the same organization working on a single business objective such as managing diversity. A second flaw in the use of consultants for knowledge transfer among organization units is that they typically have high-intensity involvement only during the launch period of change efforts and are less involved as the work progresses. For this reason any help that they give with knowledge transfer is often too short lived.

I believe that the failure to create effective mechanisms for transferring knowledge about how to manage diversity effectively is a major obstacle to the success of work in this area. Ideas on steps to address this problem can be gleaned from an application of the list of key factors for success provided in Table 7.2.

Key Success Factors of Knowledge Management

A discussion of all nine elements of Table 7.2 is beyond the scope of this book. Instead, I will briefly discuss a sample of three items: (1) senior management support, (2) the need for a culture that is supportive of sharing knowledge, and (3) the use of multiple channels.

Senior management support was emphasized in Chapter Three, where I noted that strong leadership is essential for any change effort to succeed. The axiom "get senior management support" is applied here as the first thing that needs to happen to create good knowledge management in your organization. When top leaders understand the importance of retaining and distributing knowledge as a competitive tool and when they make this a priority in their communications with their direct reports and support it with appropriate resources, the likelihood of developing an effective knowledge management process is greatly increased. The opposite is also true. When knowledge management is not a priority, or when top leaders think of it as being synonymous with having a state-of-the-art computer information system, the probability of having good knowledge management is severely reduced.

If you are in the position of understanding the power of knowledge management but are working in a firm where it is not well understood or given proper top management sponsorship, your task is to educate the top leaders so that they will get behind an effort to make knowledge management an integral part of what the firm is doing as a follow-up step in your managing diversity effort. If your organization is like Booz•Allen & Hamilton and has someone assigned as a knowledge management officer, then I suggest that you work to get learning on diversity included in the knowledge accumulation and distribution process that this person is responsible for overseeing. However, it is not necessary to have such a role to accomplish knowledge transfer on managing diversity. What top leaders must do is to charge someone *at the enterprise level* in the organization with coordinating the collection and dissemination of learning about how to do diversity change work well. This may be a person in HR, in a business strategy or planning group, or in information systems; or it may be a corporate diversity officer.

A second success factor for knowledge management that we can readily apply to managing diversity work is the development of a *knowledge-sharing culture.* In such an open culture, people are accustomed to a free flow of information to and from people outside their immediate work area or department that is helpful to their current projects. Unfortunately, this success factor is absent in many organizations.

Two prominent symptoms of a culture that is not supportive of sharing knowledge are the "not invented here" syndrome and the tendency to withhold information as a source of power. The latter obstacle is straightforward, and I won't elaborate on it. The "not invented here" syndrome occurs when people from one organization unit routinely reject, or simply take little interest in, ideas of other units because they represent the thinking of "outsiders." In part this mind-set comes from an assumption, which is often false, that one's own unit is unique and therefore whatever worked somewhere else is inapplicable. Another source of the "not invented here" mind-set comes from a tendency to think that we can come up with something better than what any other unit might do. This is especially true when the unit with the relevant experience has a reputation either for being very strong (jealousy obstacle) or very weak (assumed superiority obstacle).

If your organization has a culture that freely shares information across organization boundaries, this will be a major help in getting knowledge management to work. If not, you will need to do some work on culture change in the area of creating open communications in order to lay the proper groundwork for the implementation of knowledge management.

The final success factor that I will discuss is that knowledge management programs are most effective when there are *multiple channels for sharing knowledge.* This factor warrants my most extensive comments because the core issue is increasing the movement of knowledge among people in the organization. An important point to be made about this in terms of managing diversity efforts is to avoid the trap of thinking that the appointment of a corporate diversity officer alone will fulfill the need for knowledge transfer regarding the work on diversity. To achieve maximum effectiveness, you will need to do more, and if your firm is like Eli Lilly or Alcoa and does not have a corporate diversity officer role, you obviously will need to look at other means of accomplishing the tasks of accumulating information about how to do diversity work and making it accessible throughout the organization.

In line with the advice to have more than one method of facilitating the sharing of information on managing diversity, I offer three ideas that go beyond the options of leveraging a common consulting group or the diversity officer role. The first is to organize diversity conferences. These conferences bring people from various parts of the enterprise together to spend from one to three days focusing on the topic of managing diversity. Each conference should be attended by change leaders from different organizational units and, at least for certain segments, by top leaders of the units involved.

Although these conferences often feature speeches by top managers and presentations by outside consultants, a *major purpose should be for internal change agents to share learning about how to manage diversity.* To illustrate this, you will recall my earlier reference to the work of the Wenatche operation of Alcoa's Primary Metals business on workplace harassment. As a result of word-of-mouth communication about this work, the local management team was getting calls from other parts of the company asking for information on what they were doing. As a response, they decided to organize a conference on diversity for the entire business unit, with a central objective being to promote a transfer of knowledge among the units involved. Of course, care must be taken when planning such events to avoid a perception that any one unit has all the answers. Instead, the mind-set to promote is that of mutual sharing of lessons learned.

Every year there are national conferences on diversity featuring leading consultants, industry change agents, and university experts talking about ideas for effectively managing diversity. These serve a useful purpose, and I recommend attendance at carefully selected ones as a part of the development plan for people who want to raise their skill level. However, you should not underestimate the value of internal conferences, especially if your organization is large and has units that are at different stages of development in the work on diversity.

The tool of internal conferences is useful but it also has some obvious limitations, most notably that conferences are one-time or at least infrequent events. Two other ideas overcome this limitation. My second suggestion for promoting knowledge transfer is to create a computer database of knowledge on managing diversity. This is an idea that I have been trying to get Alcoa to adopt for some time. The basic plan is to develop a formal process for the recording of learning about managing diversity experiences of people across the firm and then making this learning available in a user-friendly format to anyone in the firm who needs it. The database should be organized by subtopics so that users can quickly tap into the accumulated knowledge that is most relevant to them. For example, if you have successful experience with bringing diversity into the new-hire orientation process, some highlights of what you did can be entered under a subheading of new-hire orientation. Also, contact information should be provided in case the user wants further details.

Although I have not yet seen this idea used explicitly for managing diversity information, similar databases exist in some companies for other topics. For example, Ford has a program called the "Lessons Learned" database that features information about new product development. The tremendous improvements in the availability and capabilities of information technology that have taken place in the last decade have greatly enhanced the potential value of this means for knowledge transfer, yet it remains a grossly underutilized tool for managing diversity knowledge.

The final idea for promoting knowledge transfer on managing diversity is to create a network of liaison people whose function, in part, is to provide communication linkages between units of the organization. This is not necessarily a full- or part-time position but more often a designated role for an existing employee. General Electric and Ford are two companies that have created something like this with designated diversity coordinators in various business units throughout the firm.

The existence of such a network provides a ready-made "mailing list" for the distribution of diversity-related learning and information. The network can easily be joined electronically via e-mail and maintain a stream of communication about what is going on in the various units of the organization. A sample entry might be "have found a very effective trainer on the topic of cultural differences; the person is based in . . .; for details contact. . . ." Having a network of liaison people can be a strong supplement to having a database, partly because it adds the all-important human touch to the rather sterile presentation of information that occurs on computers. My second and third ideas can be merged by having the people in the liaison network take responsibility for data entry for the managing diversity database. However, the latter task can become very demanding, and care must be taken to ensure that these employees are not over-loaded with work. I have often seen this happen and, as with all activities, managers have an obligation to balance workloads so that neither the quantity nor quality of the work on knowledge management is compromised and employees are treated fairly and with respect.

CHAPTER SUMMARY

When change efforts fail, the cause can often be traced to poor follow-up. When follow-up is poor, there is more at stake than just the inability to realize the vision for change. I believe that the integrity of leadership is severely compromised when we say that we are going to change things and then don't do it. Outlined in this chapter are four keys to good follow-up for change efforts to manage diversity: (1) use planning review processes, (2) keep score, (3) provide incentives for the new behaviors, and (4) manage the retention and transfer of knowledge. Tips for implementing each of these were given. Through attention to these four steps, accountability will be strengthened and you will greatly enhance your ability to leverage what you are learning to sustain continuous improvements of results.

Questions for Further Learning and Development

1. Who is accountable for making the change to manage diversity more effectively in your organization?
2. How strong is the accountability for managing diversity in your organization?
3. If diversity competency is considered in selection decisions in your organization, is it treated as a threshold factor or a portfolio factor? Which should it be?

    If diversity competency is not considered at all, why is this the case?

    Do you agree with the statement, When the vision for diversity is fully realized, it will be commonplace for a candidate's reputation for dealing with diversity to be discussed at length during meetings where people are being evaluated for promotion? Why or why not?

4. How well and by what means is information shared in your organization relative to lessons learned in managing diversity?

Do you have lessons learned that should be on a managing diversity database? If so, list them.

List one to three areas of knowledge where you could use some immediate help from a database on lessons learned in managing diversity.

■ Final Thoughts

When nations and their organizations espouse beliefs such as (1) people are the most valuable resource, (2) every person will be treated with dignity and respect, and (3) there will be equal employment opportunities for people of all social-cultural groups, they take upon themselves a moral obligation to fulfill these promises. For this reason the quest to create organizational excellence to manage diversity is more than a call to maximize economic performance. It is, in part, a call to bring integrity to our governments and our organizations and to the people who lead them.

Fulfilling the espoused values and beliefs of nations and organizations relating to diversity requires a combination of knowing how and commitment to follow through and do what must be done. I wrote this book as an effort to help with the first of these requirements. I have shown that although diversity in work groups presents some formidable challenges, the capacity of organizations to welcome and leverage diversity as a key resource can be improved by using a strategy involving leadership, research and measurement, education, the alignment of management systems and practices, and rigorous follow-up. Through commitment to using the strategy in a sincere effort to promote ongoing change, organizations can journey to a higher place of accomplishment and more fully capture the power of diversity.

Notes

Chapter One

1. William B. Johnston, "Global Work Force 2000: The New World Labor Market," *Harvard Business Review* (March-April 1991): 115–127.

2. William B. Johnston and Arnold H. Packer, *Workforce 2000: Work and Workers for the Twenty-First Century* (Indianapolis, Ind.: Hudson Institute; Washington, D.C.: U.S. Department of Labor, 1987).

3. For reviews and references see Taylor Cox Jr. and Ruby L. Beale, *Developing Competency to Manage Diversity: Readings, Cases & Activities* (San Francisco: Berrett-Koehler, 1997) and Kathleen Williams and Charles O'Reilly, "1998 Demography and Diversity in Organizations: A Review of 40 Years of Research," in *Research in Organizational Behavior* 20 (1997): 77–140.

4. See R. Roosevelt Thomas Jr.'s 1996 book, *Redefining Diversity* (New York: American Management Association).

5. For Nemeth's research see Charlene J. Nemeth, "Dissent, Group Process, and Creativity," *Advances in Group Processes* 2 (1985): 57–75; "Differential Contributions of Majority and Minority Influence," *Psychological Review* 93 (1986): 23–32; Charlene J. Nemeth and J. Wachter, "Creative Problem Solving as a Result of Majority Versus Minority Influence," *European Journal of Social Psychology* 13 (1983): 45–55.

6. See Harry C. Triandis, E. R. Hall, and R. B. Ewen, "Member Hetero-geneity and Dyadic Creativity," *Human Relations* 18 (1965): 33–55; Nancy Adler, *International Dimensions of Organization Behavior* (Boston: Kent Publishing, 1986).

7. Saul Siegel and William Kammerer, "Measuring the Perceived Support for Innovation in Organizations," *Journal of Applied Psychology* 63 (1978): 553–562.

8. Poppy L. McLeod, Sharon A. Lobel, and Taylor Cox Jr., "Ethnic Diversity and Creativity in Small Groups," *Small Group Research* 27 (1996): 248–264.

9. See, for example, N. G. Rotter and A. N. O'Connell, "The Relationships Among Sex-Role Orientation, Cognitive Complexity and Tolerance for Ambiguity," *Sex Roles* 8 (1982): 1209–1220; David Shaffer, Clyde Hendrick, Robert Regula, and Joseph Freconna, "Interactive Effects of Ambiguity Tolerance and Task Effort on Dissonance Reduction," *Journal of Personality* 41 (1973): 224–233.

10. See the review of this research by Wallace Lambert, "The Effects of Bilingualism on the Individual: Cognitive and Sociocultural Consequences," in P. A. Hurnbey (ed.), *Bilingualism: Psychological, Social and Educational Implications* (San Diego: Academic Press, 1977), pp. 15–27.

11. See Richard A. Levy, "Ethnic & Racial Differences in Response to Medicines: Preserving Individualized Therapy in Managed Pharmaceutical Programs" (Reston, Virginia: National Pharmaceutical Council, 1993); John A. McCarty, "Current Theory and Research on Cross-Cultural Factors in Consumer Behavior," in *Advances in Consumer Research* 16 (1989), pp. 127–129; David K. Tse, Kam-hon Lee, Illan Vertinsky, and Donald A. Wehrung, "Does Culture Matter? A Cross-Cultural Study of Executives' Choice, Decisiveness, and Risk Adjustment in International Marketing," *Journal of Marketing* 52 (October 1988): 81–85.

12. For examples of this research see the following: Taylor Cox Jr. and Joycelyn Finley, "An Analysis of Work Specialization and Organization Level as Dimensions of Workforce Diversity," in Martin Chemers, Stuart Oskamp, and Mark Costanzo (eds.), *Diversity in Organizations* (Newbury Park, Calif.: Sage, 1995): pp. 62–90; J. Barnett, "Understanding Group Effects Within Organizations: A Study of Group Atti-

tudes and Behaviors of Engineers and Scientists," (Ph.D. diss., The Fielding Institute, Santa Barbara, Calif., 1994); Sally Helgesen, *The Female Advantage: Women's Ways of Leadership* (New York: Doubleday, 1990); Deborah Tannen, *Talking from 9 to 5* (New York: Avon, 1995); Rosalie L. Tung, "People's Republic of China," in R. Nath (ed.), *Comparative Management: A Regional View* (Cambridge, Mass.: Ballinger, 1988a): pp. 139–168; Stephen B. Knouse, Paul Rosenfeld, and Amy L. Culbertson (eds.), *Hispanics in the Workplace* (Sage, 1992).

13. See the following for a detailed discussion of organizational acculturation processes: Taylor Cox Jr. and J. Finley-Nickelson, "Models of Acculturation for Intra-Organizational Cultural Diversity," *Canadian Journal of Administrative Sciences* 8 (1991): 90–100.

14. For example, see Daniel Katz and Robert Kahn, *The Social Psychology of Organizations,* 2nd ed. (New York: Wiley, 1978).

Chapter Two

1. Sara Rynes and Benson Rosen, "A Field Survey of Factors Affecting the Adoption and Perceived Success of Diversity Training," *Personnel Psychology* 48 (1995): 247–270; P. L. Nemetz and S. L. Christensen, "The Challenge of Cultural Diversity: Harnessing a Diversity of Views to Understand Multiculturalism," *Academy of Management Review* 11 (1996): 736–749.

2. Noel M. Tichy and M. A. Devanna, *The Transformational Leader,* 2nd ed. (New York: Wiley, 1990); B. M. Bass and B. J. Avolio, "The Implications of Transactional and Transformational Leadership for Individual, Team, And Organizational Development," *Research in Organizational Change and Development* (1990): 321–372.

3. L. von Bertalanffy, "The History and Status of General Systems Theory," *Academy of Management Journal* 15:4 (1972): 407–426; Daniel Katz and Robert Kahn, *The Social Psychology of Organizations.*

4. Thomas S. Kuhn, *The Structure of Scientific Revolutions: International Encyclopedia of Unified Science,* vol. II, no. 2 (Chicago: University of Chicago Press, 1970): p. 112.

5. For example, see the following work: Lennie Copeland, "Valuing Workplace Diversity," *Personnel* 33 (1988): 38–40; John W. Berry,

"Acculturation: A Comparative Analysis of Alternative Forms," in J. Samunda and S. L. Woods (eds.), *Perspectives in Immigrant and Minority Education* (Lanham, Md.: University Press of America, 1983): pp. 66–77; Gert Hofstede, *Culture's Consequences: International Differences in Work-Related Values* (Newbury Park, Calif. and London: Sage, 1980); R. Roosevelt Thomas Jr., "From Affirmative Action to Affirming Diversity," *Harvard Business Review* 68:2 (March-April 1990): 17–117; Clayton P. Alderfer and Ken K. Smith, "Studying Intergroup Relations Embedded in Organizations," *Administrative Science Quarterly* 27 (1982): 5–65; Clayton P. Alderfer and David Thomas, "The Significance of Race and Ethnicity for Understanding Organizational Behavior," in C. L. Cooper and I. Robertson (eds.), *International Review of Industrial and Organizational Psychology* (London: Wiley, 1988); Ed Jones, "Black Managers: The Dream Deferred," *Harvard Business Review* 64 (1986); Rosabeth Moss Kanter, *Men and Women of the Corporation* (New York: Basic Books, 1977); John P. Fernandez, *Managing a Diverse Workforce* (Lexington, Mass.: Lexington Books, 1991); Marilyn Loden and Judy B. Rosener, *Workforce America! Managing Employee Diversity as a Vital Resource* (Homewood, Ill.: Business One Irwin, 1991).

Chapter Three

1. B. M. Bass, "Leadership: Good, Better, Best," *Organizational Dynamics* (Winter 1985): 25–40.
2. For examples of this research see A. J. Wood and H. H. Zhou, "Ethnic Differences in Drug Disposition and Responsiveness," *Clinical Pharmacokinet* 20 (1991): 350–373; H. H. Zhou, R. P. Koshakii, D. J. Silberstein, and A. J. Wood, "Racial Differences in Response: Altered Sensitivity to and Clearance of Propranolol in Men of Chinese Descent as Compared with American Whites," *New England Journal of Medicine* 320 (1989): 565–570.

Chapter Four

1. See, for example, J. N. Cleveland and F. H. Landy, "The Effects of Person and Job Stereotypes on Two Personnel Decisions," *Journal of*

Applied Psychology 68 (1983): 609–619; B. Rosen and T. H. Jerdee, "The Influence of Age Stereotypes on Managerial Decisions," *Journal of Applied Psychology* 61:4 (1976): 428–432; Jeffrey Greenhaus and Saroj Parasuraman, "Job Performance Attributions and Career Advancement Prospects: An Examination of Gender and Race Effects," *Organizational Behavior and Human Decision Processes* 55 (1993): 273–297.

2. For more on this research see *Cultural Diversity in Organizations: Theory, Research & Practice* by Taylor Cox Jr. (San Francisco: Berrett-Koehler, 1993).

Chapter Five

1. Sara Rynes and Benson Rosen," A Field Survey of Factors Affecting the Adoption and Perceived Success of Diversity Training," *Personnel Psychology* 48 (1995): 247–270.

2. For a sample of cases to teach about diversity, see the book by Taylor Cox Jr. and Ruby L. Beale, *Developing Competency to Manage Diversity* (San Francisco: Berrett-Koehler, 1997).

3. Two such organizations are The Mad Hatters Educational Theatre Group of Kalamazoo Michigan and The Cornell University School of Dramatic Arts.

4. For information on this tool, contact my consulting office at (734) 451–9610 or e-mail us at Taylorcox@msn.com.

5. One excellent resource is *The Fifth Discipline Fieldbook* by Peter Senge and colleagues (New York: Doubleday, 1994).

Chapter Six

1. For examples of research supporting this point see Jane L. Swanson, "Life-Span Career Development and Reciprocal Interaction of Work and Nonwork," *Journal of Vocational Behavior* 41:2 (1992): 101–161; Jack Kammer, *Good Will Toward Men* (New York: St. Martin's Press, 1994).

2. See, for example, Robert Henneman, Nancy Waldeck, and Michele Cushnie, "Diversity Considerations in Staffing Decision-Making," in

□

Managing Diversity: Human Resource Strategies for Transforming the Workplace, Ellen Kossek and Sharon Lobel (eds.) (Cambridge, Mass.: Blackwell, 1996): pp. 74–102.

3. For example, see a discussion of some of this research and some empirical findings in the article "Race, Gender, and Opportunity: A Study of Compensation Attainment and the Establishment of Mentoring Relationships," by George Dreher and Taylor Cox Jr., *The Journal of Applied Psychology* 81 (1996): 297–308.

4. For example, see the work of George Dreher and Taylor Cox Jr., "Labor Market Mobility and Salary Attainment: The Moderating Effects of Race and Gender," *Academy of Management Journal* 43 (2000), 890–901; also see David Thomas, "The Impact of Race on Manager's Experiences of Developmental Relationships," *The Journal of Organizational Behavior* 11 (1990): 479–492.

5. For examples of research that addresses differential access to informal networks see Herminia Ibarra, "Race, Opportunity and Diversity of Social Circles in Managerial Networks," *Academy of Management Journal* 38 (1995): 673–703; D. J. Brass, "Men's and Women's Networks: A Study of Interaction Patterns and Influence in an Organization," *Academy of Management Journal* 28 (1985): 327–343; Ann M. Morrison and Mary Ann Von Glinow, "Women and Minorities in Management," *American Psychologist* 45 (1990): 200–208.

6. For example, Nancy Adler (*International Dimensions of Organizational Behavior,* Kent Publishing, 1996) is among those who have written about both the high level of learning potential inherent in expatriate assignments and the tendency of multinationals to underutilize their learning to develop skills in other people when the expatriate returns home.

Chapter Seven

1. See McClelland's book, *The Achieving Society* (New York: Van Nostrand Reinhold, 1961), as well as his book, *Human Motivation* (Glenview, Ill.: Scott Foresman, 1985).

2. For example, see the classic work on the theory of organization behavior modification by W. C. Hamner and E. P. Hamner, "Behavior

Modification on the Bottom Line," *Organizational Dynamics* 4 (1976): 8–21, and on expectancy theory such as Victor H. Vroom, *Work and Motivation* (New York: Wiley, 1964).

3. For a discussion of this point see Simon Trussler's article, "The Rules of the Game," *Journal of Business Strategy* (January-February 1998): 16–17.

4. See Thomas Davenport and Laurence Prusak, *How Organizations Manage What They Know* (Boston: Harvard Business School Press, 1998).

5. This is based on the following reference: Thomas H. Davenport, Sirkka L. Jarvenpaa, and Michael C. Beers, "Improving Knowledge Work Processes," *Sloan Management Review* (Summer 1997): 53–65.

The Author

Taylor Cox Jr. is associate professor of organizational behavior and human resource management at the University of Michigan Business School, where he teaches courses on organizational diagnosis and consulting, cultural diversity in organizations, and human resources as a competitive advantage. He is also founder and president of Taylor Cox and Associates, Inc., a research and consulting firm specializing in organization change and development work for clients with culturally diverse workforces and markets.

Taylor is the author or coauthor of more than twenty-five published articles and cases. His book, *Cultural Diversity in Organizations: Theory, Research & Practice,* was the 1994 co-winner of the prestigious George R. Terry Book Award, given by the National Academy of Management to the book contributing the most to the advancement of the state of knowledge in management during the previous two years.

His consulting has included strategic planning, research, educational programs, and human resource systems alignment with more than twenty organizations, including Alcoa, Exxon, Ford Motor Company, Phelps Dodge, General Electric, Eli Lilly, and the Ohio State University.

Index